Ronnie Maasz was a
resident of Wiveliscombe.

Please return/renew this item
by the last date shown.

# FILMMAKERS SERIES
## edited by
## ANTHONY SLIDE

103. *Perpetually Cool: The Many Lives of Anna May Wong (1905–1961)*, by Anthony B. Chan. 2003
104. *Irene Dunne: The First Lady of Hollywood*, by Wes D. Gehring. 2003
105. *Scorsese Up Close: A Study of the Films*, by Ben Nyce. 2003
106. *Hitchcock and Poe: The Legacy of Delight and Terror*, by Dennis R. Perry. 2003
107. *Life Is Beautiful, but Not for Jews*, by Kobi Niv, translated by Jonathan Beyrak Lev. 2003
108. *Young Man in Movieland*, by Jan Read. 2003
109. *A Cast of Shadows*, by Ronnie Maasz. 2004.

# A Cast of Shadows

Ronnie Maasz

*Filmmakers Series, No. 109*

THE SCARECROW PRESS, INC.
Lanham, Maryland, and Oxford
2004

SCARECROW PRESS, INC.

Published in the United States of America
by Scarecrow Press, Inc.
A wholly owned subsidary of
The Rowman & Littlefield Publishing Group, Inc.
4501 Forbes Boulevard, Suite 200, Lanham, Maryland 20706
www.scarecrowpress.com

PO Box 317
Oxford
OX2 9RU, UK

British Library Cataloguing in Publication Information Available

**Library of Congress Cataloging-in-Publication Data**

Maasz, Ronnie.
     A cast of shadows / Ronnie Maasz.
          p. cm. — (Filmmakers series ; no. 109)
     Includes index.
     ISBN 0-8108-4883-X (alk. paper)
     1. Maasz, Ronnie. 2. Cinematographers—England—Biography. I. Title.
II. Series.
TR849.M33 .A3 2004
778.5'3'092—dc21                                                        2003011921

∞™ The paper used in this publication meets the minimum requirements of
American National Standard for Information Sciences—Permanence of Paper for
Printed Library Materials, ANSI/NISO Z39.48-1992.
Manufactured in the United States of America.

To all the talented people I have worked with over the years—all my colleagues and fellow workers in this unique business. I hope they have had as much fun, enjoyment, and a sense of achievement as I have had.

And to my family, for not letting me slacken in the task—especially to my wife, Helen, whose support and contributions were invaluable.

~

# Contents

.

~

# Preface

The low autumn sunlight angled across the road, picking up the swirling dust as it moved over the cars. Above the traffic noise, a steady thumping could be heard. The car in front had stopped, and some hundred yards ahead the red gleam of a traffic light was accentuated by the refracting dust. I slowed to a halt and glanced to my right through a line of poplar trees. The sunlight played on a huge crane partially obscured by the green foliage, a large metal ball dangling from it that thumped hard against a tall white plastered wall. I suddenly realized what I was looking at. Denham Studios—or what remained of it . . .

It was 1942, and I was gingerly carrying a large metal tray of overfilled tea cups—slopping onto the tray brought from the canteen at the top of the quarter-mile-long corridor that ran the whole length of the studios—and emerging squinting in the bright light of the set of *The Great Mr. Handel*, the story of the composer's sojourn in London as Master of the King's Musick. I was not aware then that it was being photographed in three-strip Technicolor by Claude Friese Green, son of the famous man himself, and that the Technicolor consultant was Jack Cardiff, who was just beginning his illustrious career. Nor did I know that the camera operator was another man destined to be a world-class cameraman himself—Geoffrey Unsworth. A Cockney voice said, "See the tide's aht agin!" and a hand indicated the tea lake in the tray. Another voice shouted through the din, "Watch your arc, Bert. It's flickering," and a reply came from somewhere above: "Wot dy'er mean? I bin in this game for twenty years and ain't never ever 'ad a flicker!" Through the extremely hot arc-laden atmosphere—it was Technicolor's early slow film days—a perspiring property man dragging a heavy table passed by, catching the tea tray and spilling some over the edge: "Sorry, me old son. . . ."

The sound of a car horn disturbed my reverie, and I became aware that the car that had been in front was now a hundred yards away, a green light glinting through the dust. I cast a last backward look. Memories. . . .

This is an autobiographical tale of fifty years in the film business. It consists, in part, of the many films I was involved in, the people and characters I met making them, and the places I went to make them.

Film technicians are the last of the "traveling players." They travel worldwide to set up their tents and ply their trade. The film industry is unique in that you never know where you may find yourself next week, or even next day, for that matter. And the bonus is that you get to see the world at someone else's expense (usually). Sometimes you spend long periods in one place and make new friends, some of which endure and some that are simply "ships that pass in the night." Other times you rush from place to place, hardly seeing your surroundings, living in hotels and out of a suitcase, and knowing only the road to and from the airport. And you can find yourself sleeping in the most unlikely places. I once slept on a plank bed in the cell of an African police station, there being no other accommodation available.

Much has been made of the alleged "glamor" of the film business. In reality, it is a tough, highly competitive industry in which security—particularly financial—is not easy to come by. It is also imperative that you possess a sense of humor, invaluable at all times. Personally I consider myself very fortunate to have been a part of it, working with so many talented people.

~

# Acknowledgments

It would be very remiss of me not to acknowledge the people with whom I worked and learnt so much about cinematography, and who also became my friends. So my grateful thanks to Robert Krasker, B.S.C.; John Wilcox, B.S.C.; Oswald Morris, B.S.C. and O.B.E.; Freddie Frances, B.S.C.; Freddie Young, B.S.C. and O.B.E., and not a few others. I owe them all a great debt.

# CHAPTER 1

~

# In the Beginning

I have never thought it desirable to dwell for very long on the beginning of anyone's career. The details are not usually of the greatest interest, and in my case I doubt that many people would really want to know, with the possible exception of my aged Aunt Ada. Even after my forty years–plus as a freelance cameraman, she is still very concerned that I do not seem able to "hold down a job for any length of time." Repeated attempts to explain the workings of the business have met with incomprehension. She appears to think that I am one of a band of itinerant "strolling players."

Most of my contemporaries have admitted to being fascinated by film at an early age, but apart from a vague interest it was not paramount to my young life. I did, however, have an inquisitive interest in photography, and with the aid of an ancient "box Brownie" contributed by an uncle, I spent a lot of time photographing anything in sight in what I presumed was an interesting and innovative manner. I rigged up a makeshift darkroom under the stairs to do the processing and attempted to critique my weird and wonderful efforts. In common with many young boys about to leave school, I had no real idea what I wanted to do in life.

My father was understanding and informed me that I could try anything I liked—within reason, of course—but he would like to see me "settled" by the time I was twenty-one. Fortunately he did have an old friend who was the construction manager at the famous Ealing Studios and he asked him to look out for a possible job vacancy there. The opportunity came fairly quickly as it was 1941 and the studio personnel were rapidly being conscripted into the armed forces. To my delight, a job came up in the camera department, and I was interviewed and accepted.

To the uninitiated, entering a film studio for the first time is quite an experience. Years of "going to the pictures" gives you an anticipation of something novel and far removed from everyday life. You expect to see a world of exciting artifice. After passing through the front gate you are confronted with the usual disheveled order of the normal studio, pieces of discarded sets, piles of sweepings and heaps of scaffolding and wooden planks. And you suddenly become aware of the Smell. It is common to every film studio in the world. I don't think that it has ever been fully analyzed, but it seems to be an amalgam of wet plaster, size, paint, and film stock, among other things. Whatever it is, it is quite unique and you never forget it.

My first job in the camera department was learning the mechanics of the cine camera and the mandatory tasks of floor sweeping and tea fetching. The cameras were American-made N. C. Mitchells. They were far from new but had been well maintained and, as they were efficiently designed and built, were capable of a long life. Ealing had never been one of the wealthy studios, and it tended to use all its equipment for as long as it held together. The "blimps" the camera was housed in for sound purposes needed constant repair to the inside insulation, and the heads on which the blimp was mounted were ancient and also in need of constant maintenance.

The majority of the camera equipment was held together by "chewing gum and string," but it sufficed, and I think they carried on that way all through the war. Ealing did manage to make some highly acclaimed pictures with it. Getting replacement parts gradually became more difficult in wartime, but the chief mechanic, a genial man named George Burrows, was able to manufacture small parts that could not be obtained elsewhere at all. He was a very hard taskmaster but was patient and kindly with me, and a good teacher.

Once settled in to the camera department, I started to discover who was who, and who did what. I learned that the overall boss was the director of photography, the man responsible for all the lighting and the visuals. Next in line was the camera operator who did exactly that and was also the director of photography's right-hand man. He arranged the composition—with the DOP—and was responsible for everything in front of the camera, and in the days before video assist was also the director's "eyes." It was a very responsible job and a very rewarding one.

Then came the first assistant cameraman, generally known as the "focus puller." His job was to ensure that the actors or objects were kept "sharp" by following the lens focus when the subject or the camera was moving. He was also in charge of the mechanics of the camera and all its ancillary equipment. And then there was the lowliest member—the second assistant cameraman, the clapper/loader who loaded and unloaded the film, kept the records, and placed the number board in front of the camera for every shot—and the general gofer. My next promotion had me serving in that capacity.

I was allocated to the crew making *Went the Day Well,* a wartime story of the invasion of Germans, dressed in British Army uniforms, on a small country village. We went on location to a village in Buckinghamshire some thirty miles from London.

Up to that point I had been confined to the maintenance room and had had a fairly low profile. But now I was exposed to all the vagaries of filmmaking and working with a large number of people, which I was not used to. My responsibilities and other people's obvious expectations diminished what little confidence I had. But the crew were kind, knowing my inexperience, and many of them gave me advice—some of which I subsequently learned was not particularly accurate, but it was undoubtedly well meant. It was very hot weather and a ten-hour day toiling up and down the hills carrying the heavy camera equipment meant that I slept very soundly at night. As I gained more confidence I realized that I was thoroughly enjoying myself. And my enthusiasm for this filmmaking grew with it. This was the career I wanted.

I continued in the post of clapper/loader for another three or four productions but, because of the escalation of military conscription, I was promoted relatively quickly to the next grade, that of first assistant (focus) cameraman. I was far too inexperienced to be put on a crew making a major movie, but I was allowed to do "artiste's tests" and exteriors as part of my on-the-job training. In American film parlance "screen tests," they were an essential part of filmmaking then. Even eminent people were tested in front of the camera to see whether they were right for the part or not and to see how they photographed. Makeup, hair styles, and costumes were tested as well.

Then came a lull in production at Ealing Studios that fortunately coincided with a period of activity at Gainsborough Pictures studio in Shepherds Bush, London. I was sent there under a mutual agreement between the two companies on a form of permanent loan.

So the next phase began.

# CHAPTER 2

~

# The Gainsborough Lady

Going to Shepherds Bush studios was to prove a milestone in my life. Here I was to meet many people who were to become lifelong friends—and to learn a lot more about making films.

Gainsborough was responsible for a number of pictures made during the war years that attained universal acclaim. Titles like *The Wicked Lady*, *The Man in Grey*, *Christopher Columbus* (the first version starring Fredric March, and also the first film in three-strip Technicolor made by the company), *The Way to the Stars*, *Jassy*, and on and on. It had under contract players such as Margaret Lockwood, Phyllis Calvert, James Mason, and Stewart Granger, big names in the British cinema of that era. Its screen trademark was a portrait of a beautiful lady in a long period dress with a large brimmed hat. She inclined her head in gracious acknowledgment, hence the "Gainsborough Lady."

The camera equipment at Shepherds Bush was in better shape than at Ealing. The cameras were also Mitchells, but there were more of them and they were in generally better condition. The head of the camera department and chief mechanic was George Hill. George was another improviser who, as the war progressed, built bits for the cameras as they became unobtainable. A small man who had shaking hands, he could nonetheless be highly efficient when dealing with instrument screws and screwdrivers. He was very proud of the members of his department, whom he always referred to as "my boys."

My first assignment was on *Waterloo Road,* which featured John Mills, Stewart Granger, Alastair Sim, and Jean Kent. It was written and directed by Sydney Gilliat, who went on to make many successful movies, including the famous *St. Trinian's* series. I was to work with Sydney again much later on. He was another genial man who was very easy to work with.

Trains and railway stations featured largely in the story. I was the "focus-puller" on the second unit, which meant leaping around and all over the London Waterloo terminal. The second unit was especially designed to allow the main unit to carry on with the story and the actors. Today it is quite common practice and is usually referred to as the "action" unit. A Southern Railway manager, who spent the entire time utterly bewildered, officially supervised our proceedings. He obviously thought that we were prime candidates for the nearest mental institution. We photographed trains going in and out of the station in all weather conditions from bridges and platforms and alongside the line. We did "points of view" shots from the engine cab itself. We shot back projection plates from inside the moving carriages and on the platform. We climbed up onto the high roof of the station to get an establishing long shot.

At the end of three weeks we had exhausted the potential of Waterloo station. After seeing it all on the screen Sydney Gilliat said dryly "Well, I don't think you have left anything out."

I loved the atmosphere at Gainsborough. It was more relaxed and informal than Ealing had been—and I was earning one pound sterling more than I had been there. I was also now participating in things that to date had been a closed book to me—like back projection and the essentials of getting the right lighting balance between the actors in the foreground and screen with the background projected plate—and the restrictions that process placed on camera and actors' movements.

I also learned about models. After *Waterloo Road* I was assigned to a cameraman named Jack Whitehead, whose specialty was shooting miniature ships and structures so that they looked lifesize. He was a law unto himself and was left entirely to his own devices. I would be in the studio at the usual time of 8:00 A.M., but Jack seldom showed up until after lunch—and on many occasions, later.

He also took his time in actually shooting the models. If it was at all complicated we sometimes did not roll the camera until midnight. Many a night I had to sleep in one of the dressing rooms, there being no public transport then available to get me home. But I got something out of it. I learned a lot about photographing models, little realizing how useful that knowledge would be in later years.

J. Arthur Rank had added the two studios at Shepherds Bush and Islington to his film empire during the war, but in 1948 he decided to concentrate all production at the studios at Denham and Pinewood and close the others, including Shepherds Bush. Some longtime employees were transferred, but I, being a comparative newcomer, was not.

I had, perforce, to look elsewhere if I wished to continue my career in films.

# CHAPTER 3

~

# The World Outside

After the relatively safe and familiar atmosphere of Shepherds Bush studios, attempting to continue my chosen career outside in an alien world may have seemed, in light of immediately subsequent happenings, a trifle rash. But perseverance paid off, and I soon learned that contacts were the essence of it all. So I beavered about, ringing studios, production companies, and the few people I knew and was getting to know at the watering holes frequented by film technicians. Most of them were at the same game, nursing half-pints of beer and keeping their ears to the ground. But we exchanged information, some of which was very helpful.

In one of the Wardour Street bars I met up with Tony Young. He had been at Gainsborough when I was, but I had only met him, briefly. Gifted with an amusing personality, he moved around what can only be described as the lower end of the business and knew quite a lot of people who were trying to set up small productions, and in his own way he was quite an organizer. At one stage he and I and another camera assistant shared an apartment in Pimlico, West London. This proved a little fraught from time to time, as the landlady was of uncertain temperament and given to the bottle and, when under the influence, endeavored to have her carnal way with us lads.

This was all right, up to a point, but she was well stricken in years and no raving beauty to boot. In the end we were forced to look for alternative accommodation.

Tony involved me in *Waving Palms*, a tale of fortune-telling backed by a gentlemen whose financial sources were a trifle suspect, to put it mildly. His main motive, we discovered, was that his lady friend wanted to be a film star. It was never destined to be a success, as the talents of the lady in question obviously lay elsewhere, and her dependence on alcohol did not improve matters. After a week of awful "dailies," stormy scenes, and tantrums, the project was finally abandoned. We did manage to get paid, however, by dint of a little pressure on the very reluctant backer. A slightly embittered crew member suggested that the film should really have been called *The Street of Waving Palms, Where It's Shady on Both Sides*.

This was followed by another fiasco entitled, very aptly, *Ice Follies*. Made partly on an ice rink in the suburbs of London and the rest at a small, indescribably dirty studio just up the road, it also was destined never to grace the silver screen. Halfway through the second week's shooting, the camera equipment was retrieved by the rental company, as the initial down payment had not been forthcoming as promised by the producer. Any financial recompense due to us also turned out not to be available. A pint of beer was the only reward of a heated discussion in a nearby bar with the supposed moneyman. I began to doubt the wisdom of my choice of career.

After another couple of incidents of a like nature and just as I was wondering whether to alter my direction in life, salvation arrived: I was offered a legitimate, properly paid job at Shepperton Studios on a feature film. Things started to look up—only just in time.

In my narrow experience this represented a big-budget movie. Entitled *The Good Die Young*, it featured such illustrious Hollywood names as Richard Baseheart, John Ireland, and Gloria Grahame. I was very impressed by their professionalism. They had obviously been trained in the technique of movie making and behaved accordingly. This was a far cry from *Waving Palms* and *Ice Follies*. Proper filmmaking and with a reasonable recompense! I could at last pay my way without worrying where the next meal was coming from.

I even bought my first car. It had an uncertain disposition and needed to be started by a crank handle; it often rendered me a physical wreck before I even got to the studio. But it did give me a sense of independence.

Shepperton Studios had an atmosphere completely different from that of any other studio I had previously worked in. Its size and its countryside location around an old manor house may have had some bearing on it, but the whole place exuded a grand manner. It had been built in the 1930s by Sir Alexander Korda, a man who always thought BIG. I was to do a lot of work there in the coming years, and wherever I subsequently went in the world it was always my home studio. There was a great camaraderie there.

After a couple of pictures I got to know all the electricians and the standbys (the carpenters, painters, prop-men, stagehands, etc.), and of course they all came to know me. If I went away for a while, going back there was like coming home. Even today, when it has been drastically altered and all those familiar faces long gone, the magic is still there.

After *The Good Die Young*, an ex-Gainsborough cameraman, Gordon Lang, offered me a picture with a location in France named *Innocents in Paris*. This was a good old English comedy, with a cast consisting of Laurence Harvey, Alastair Sim, Margaret Rutherford, and Claire Bloom. But it was a marvelous experience. Four weeks in "The City of Light," all expenses paid!

I always look back on that location with great fondness. It was high summer, Paris was all that I hoped it would be, and I stayed on the Left Bank where all the best and brightest of Parisian life was happening. We were there for "Quatorze Juillet," Bastille Day, and enjoyed French hospitality to the full. I even got to the famous Folies Bergères. For one of my tender years, all this was wonderful. The month flew by and all too soon we were back in England to shoot the studio interiors.

The business seemed to perking up a little, and quite a few feature films were being made. Next I was asked to work in Spain on *That Lady*. The director of photography was Robert Krasker.

Bob had won an Oscar for his atmospheric black-and-white photography of *The Third Man*. Always a most modest and self-deprecating man, he used the Oscar as a doorstop; I didn't see it grace his mantelpiece until much later. He was also a brilliant color cameraman. The visual images of the Italian-made *Romeo and Juliet* that he had photographed the previous year were superb and will forever remain in my memory. From him I learned a great deal.

CinemaScope had just arrived, and *That Lady* was only the second film in that format to be made in England. In those days it required two focus pullers (first assistant cameramen), because the photographing lens and the "squeezing" lens were two separate entities. Later they were combined into one.

Since none of us had used this format before, it was decided to get Nicolas Roeg to operate the "squeezing" lens, or Hypergonar, its technical name. Nic had done it on *Knights of the Round Table*, made earlier that year at MGM, and was the only one who had had any practical experience with it. Twentieth Century Fox, whose film it was, sent us a thick document explaining the best way to use this "letter box" shape.

As it turned out, the document was soon discarded. Nic made much of being the "CinemaScope expert," and made great capital out of it. But after shooting tests it became apparent that the process was not as complicated as we had initially thought. Nic, of course, had known that all along, thoroughly enjoying himself. Then a member of the MGM Camera Department, Nic later went on to be a successful cameraman and an acclaimed director.

The principal actors in *That Lady* were Olivia de Havilland and Gilbert Roland, both delightful people to work with. Roland had been a "silent" star and was very informative on old Hollywood over the dinner table. There was also some amusing rivalry between the two actors, Christopher Lee and Tony Dawson, which surfaced on location in Spain.

In the film, Chris and Tony were playing rivals, requiring a lot of horse riding and swordplay, at which each fancied himself better than the other. They played the "one upmanship" game continuously. In a bullring in El Escorial, just outside Madrid, we were shooting a sequence where Dawson as the fearless toreador had to ride into the ring displaying his superb horsemanship. The horse, unfortunately, had a mind of its own and bucked, depositing Dawson on the hard ground. He lay there moaning and groaning and making great play of it in true actor's style. Chris Lee, who was not working that day but had come along to watch the proceedings, pushed his way through the crowd surrounding him.

He solemnly regarded the writhing figure of his fellow thespian and said in a loud voice, "Nothing trivial, I hope?"

This arrested Mr. Dawson in mid-groan, and he glared as Chris smiled and strolled casually away. That round to Lee.

*That Lady* was the first of many films I was to make at MGM Studios, Boreham Wood. But what was to follow was an entirely different experience.

# CHAPTER 4

~

# A Very Different Approach

In the 1950s film production was mainly around London, although there were some small studios in the provinces. One such was in Manchester in the northwest of England. It was a disused church and was the headquarters and production center of Mancunian Films, whose proprietor was John E. Blakeley. It was known locally as "The Fun Factory." I was invited by a cameraman I had worked with at Ealing Studios, Ernest Palmer, to join his crew there.

It was filmmaking the likes of which arguably could not be found anywhere else, the whole procedure being a vaudeville turn in itself. The budgets were minimal and the script (such as it was), basic. It was little more than a series of sketches with a vague interlinking plot. On opening the script, the first thing that met the eye was *L.S. Factory Interior. Enter three comics.* Diagonally across the rest of the page was the one word, writ large, *BUSINESS.*

The performers, headed by Frank Randle, then did their act plus a little improvisation roughly pertaining to the plot. It was pure photographed Music Hall. The northern audiences loved it all.

The sparse sets were dressed with whatever could be supplied by the family or acquired from other sources at little or no cost. Such parsimony occasionally led to problems, as when Mrs. Blakeley demanded the return of her living-room furniture that she had only loaned for one day. The shoot was to have gone into a second day but was thwarted by the arrival of the irate lady herself, demanding the immediate return of her furniture because she had a very important meeting in her house that morning. I soon perceived that this was a fairly normal procedure that prompted nothing more than a quick adjustment of the schedule; the missing sequence was transferred to another set and day.

A more unlikely film director than John Blakeley was hard to imagine. He wore, with red braces, trousers rolled up above his ankles, no jacket, and a homburg. When the cameras were rolling he would exhort the comics to "Get on with it, lads!" This from a production chair that he seldom left all day. His actual technical knowledge of filmmaking was virtually nil, but what he did know was what his audiences would find amusing, and that was all that mattered.

Quite often a set would not be ready in time and a completely new sequence would have to be devised. This tended to throw the organization somewhat, but not for long. There was another unfinished set on the next stage that consisted of a flight of stairs leading nowhere. There was nothing in the script about a flight of stairs, but time must not be wasted. The comics would be summoned.

"Think of some funny gags, lads! We've got to shoot a couple of minutes of screen time here. But I don't want any blue jokes about fresh lettuce, or touching up Frank with a lighted candle. We did that last week!" A scenario was hastily flung together. It consisted of Frank returning home late from the public house slightly the worse for drink and being soundly admonished by his wife. While she's chasing him up and down the stairs he loses his false teeth. That, basically, was it, but they made great play of it, much to Blakeley's delight, and the necessary screen time was made. Hardly sophisticated material—in fact, slapstick—but just what was wanted.

If one possessed a sense of the ridiculous, the general proceedings were often hilarious. The whole setup was a Music Hall sketch in itself. One of the comics, Dan Young, who always wore a boiler suit and top hat, was the scapegoat for anything that went wrong. Even if Frank Randle accidentally tripped over something, Young would be severely berated by Blakeley for getting in his way. And, of course, he often got his lines (such as they were) wrong, whereupon the rest of the cast would leap on him. It sometimes gave one the feeling that it had all been carefully rehearsed.

All the comics that made up the Blakeley Repertory company were characters, but Frank Randle was a trifle eccentric, to put it mildly. Even Blakeley was heard to remark that "our Frank was a bit silly in the head." He had a habit of taking out his false teeth, which he usually kept in an old rubber tobacco pouch, and declaiming at large, mostly in the canteen at lunchtime. He informed his captive audience, variously, that the Russians were coming, or that the end of the world was nigh, or, as on one splendid occasion, that the studio was about to be struck and demolished by lightning. Failing that, some Act of God would do for us all.

Blakeley's number two son, John, who was officially head of the camera department, had aspirations to be a cameraman, a career he was singularly unsuited for. His technical knowledge was little in advance of his father's, but he was in charge of the old Vinten Studio cameras that the Blakeley organization possessed. Never the best even when new, they frequently gave trouble of varying descriptions, sometimes causing long holdups. However, he had acquired a surface expertise with them and with the aid of the camera assistant somehow got them going again, at least until the next time. On odd occasions he was used as the second camera operator, usually making a terrible hash of it. Normally the main camera operator (one Harold Britten) was brought from London with the rest of the crew, but on one film John prevailed upon his father to let him do the job. He managed to survive for a few days until a scene had to be shot in the Sale Lido, a local swimming pool. It consisted of Frank Randle, clad in a striped Edwardian bathing costume, capering about on the top diving board before losing his balance and falling thirty feet into the water. John was supposed to follow him with his camera but his reactions were not of the swiftest, and things did not go according to plan. His father inquired as to how the shot had worked.

"Come on, what happened?"

John shuffled his feet. "Well, er, er, Dad, he left me with an empty picture."

Father regarded him for a moment, aware that his junior offspring had done it again. "It's no good," he said. "We shall 'ave to send for

'Al." And send for 'Al they did, while poor John was once more relegated to the back row. His father obviously despaired of him.

It was all very rich material on which one could dine out. The films themselves, I was reliably informed, made a lot of money in the north of the country, if not exactly breaking the box office in London.

It would be very difficult to find a more unique method of filmmaking, and it did not move me far along my learning curve—at least technically—but it was great fun while it lasted.

As a friend of mine commented: "Well, it's all part of life's rich tapestry, I suppose!"

CHAPTER 5

~

# The Reality of the Business

By now filmmaking was my life, and I was loving every moment of it. I had also learned quite a lot. However, the actual "setting up" of a movie was something of a mystery to me and, for that matter, still is. It was not my department; someone else dealt with that.

I had gradually become aware that, unwittingly, the film business was altering my entire lifestyle. Traveling around the world to far-flung places, living in quality hotels, sampling different cuisines, mingling with big names, was heady stuff. And it was very easy to be seduced by it all. It became very necessary from time to time to bring myself back to earth and realize that I still had to live—pay my rent, feed myself, etc.—when I wasn't working, just like everybody else. Although I was quite well paid when working, it was very easy to acquire a taste for living beyond my means. Not long before, I had been paid the then going rate for a first camera assistant—hardly a fortune. Even though things had improved a bit, the tendency to have a champagne taste with a cider income, as the expression goes, was a danger, particularly for one with the sybaritic tendencies that I had. But at that time work was plentiful, so. . . .

Generally speaking, filmmaking was a more organized and leisurely business then. In the studio we worked a five-day week (8:30 A.M. to

6:00 P.M.), and the schedules were longer in general than they are to-day. And there was much more professionalism around. We were not called to satisfy the capacious maw of television just yet.

Because we were so close to the everyday workings of the business we tended to forget how the general public saw it all. When, on the odd occasion, friends or family members prevailed upon someone to invite them to the set or location, it was fascinating to hear their comments. "What do all those people actually do?" That had to be explained carefully. As someone once said to me, "I can never see a film now without thinking of all those people standing behind the camera!" And some visitor would always ask, "Why did you have to shoot that scene so many times?" We would explain that filmmaking is teamwork. There are many things that can go wrong. On the camera alone, mishaps can befall the timing of the movement, the operator covering the action properly, the focus puller making sure that the things that should be sharp in the picture actually are. That's aside from getting the actors to hit their previously positioned marks, so as to ensure that they are correctly composed in the picture. Not to mention the weather, and matching the light. Or a lamp failing at a crucial moment. And just when you think that you have that one in the can, the continuity girl points out that our hero has omitted a crucial plot line from his last speech, so we will have to go again.

The director had thought that the performances were fine. The director of photography was pleased as there had been no lighting problems. The camera crew were happy as the actors had hit their marks and the camera movement had been perfect. The sound mixer had been satisfied, but. . . . It can be rather taxing on the nervous system, particularly as, for your part, you feel it will never be as good again. But that's the movie business.

Still, nerves often do come into it, especially when skills and experience earn a promotion. A camera assistant may have worked with the same operator for some time. I was a first assistant cameraman for ten years or so before I was offered a "break" as an operator. During that time I had carefully watched the operator at work, had seen the results on the screen, and was supremely confident that I could do the job standing on my head—until the fatal day arrived. I found myself looking through the camera (or gazing down the viewfinder, as we did in those days), hearing the assistant director shout "Ready camera? Roll'em!" and being suddenly aware that from now on it is all up to me, and feeling very much on my own.

I well remember that baptism on *Reach for Glory*, a story shot in Suffolk, England, and directed by a delightful man, Phil Leacock. I was very lucky to have had Phil as my first director. A more ruthless character could easily have ruined what little confidence I then had, possibly forever. As it was, that first shot was on a "baby" crane tracking along and lifting over two boys running. It was not really too difficult, but the first two takes were not very clear in my mind. Fortunately both of them had been no good for the sound man. By take three I had more or less conquered my nerves and got it right.

The worst part was waiting to see the dailies the following evening. It's wise to get a good night's sleep before such an event. I didn't.

Sitting in the local cinema next day waiting to view the first day's work was purgatory. At last the first shot was shown. By mistake the laboratories had printed take two, which had been no good for sound. I had remembered very little of it at the time but by some miracle it was perfect. So was the third take, which I had remembered. Phil Leacock said, "Very good!" and the DOP, Bob Huke, patted me on the back. I remember thinking, "Well, they haven't fired me yet, but why didn't I stick to pulling focus?"

But once I had grasped it properly, operating the camera seemed to me arguably one of the most satisfying jobs in the film business.

Location shooting presents its own problems. The production department has to arrange to feed and shelter a mob of people for *x* number of weeks. Experienced technicians have seen most of it before, and the unit just gets on with the job at hand. The local reaction is another story. The influx of sometimes over a hundred people into a small community is not always beneficial. The sums of money being spent are good for the local economy, but even that can have tragic consequences.

The very first English location I went on was in a small Oxfordshire village in southern England, Turville Heath. We shot for the first week on a hill overlooking the village. From there we could see the thatched roof and whitewashed walls of the Bull and Butcher, the village public house. It was purely an ale house, and as it was a hot summer, the unit consumed large amounts after the day's work. The landlord was constantly ordering up fresh supplies from the nearby brewery.

On our last night he threw a party and admitted that he had had a very profitable time during our six-week sojourn. It was not until we were back in the studio that we heard that he had subsequently run amok, killed his family with an axe, and then hanged himself. And it was generally surmised that the film unit had caused the tragedy. The sudden influx of comparative wealth had proved too much.

Fortunately there are not many incidents of that nature, but film units often tend to disturb the even tenor of ways. The community is seldom quite the same again. Marriages are arranged, and babies born—often without the benefit of clergy. People leave to see if they can find something as interesting and lucrative in another town or city. The temporary surge of money can have a variety of effects, unsettling if not drastic. The film unit may be welcomed with open arms, but often its departure is just as welcome.

In fact, sometimes the production companies are guilty of misrepresenting their requirements and intentions. The owners of a house or grounds in which a company wishes to shoot a film understandably wonder what will be involved. They are usually assured that there won't be all that many people and no more equipment than necessary. They are none too pleased to find about a hundred or so people, plus trucks, generators, vans, heavy lights, and so forth, swarming all over the property and ruining the lawns and grounds. I have been present on more than one occasion when even the offer of extra money and a personal introduction to the star of the piece were not sufficient to keep us from being ignominiously ejected from the location, thereby creating a fresh set of problems. And it was entirely the production company's fault. They were trying to "get away with it."

These days I think it has all improved a bit. The general public are more aware, and the film companies a lot more responsible.

As they should.

# CHAPTER 6

~

# Bluey

The very nature of the film business attracts many types of people from all walks of life and inevitably yields up some fascinating characters. There are far too many to even attempt to recall them all, but they range across the working spectrum of the business from stagehands to producers.

One such was "Bluey" Hill. He was Australian, large and redheaded, hence the sobriquet. I don't think anyone ever knew his Christian name. He was primarily a first assistant director, but he had acted as production manager and location manager, among other roles, when called upon. At one stage he almost became a producer.

I first met him at Ealing, where we both played for its cricket team. He was their demon fast bowler, not terribly accurate but pretty lethal. I used to bowl in tandem with him, offering up innocuous "spinners." On its own merit my bowling was unlikely to be particularly successful, but after an over or two of Bluey's bullet-like deliveries, the opposition was sometimes demoralized enough to succumb to one of my relatively harmless offerings.

The principal job of a first assistant director is to be in charge of the shooting crew. Bluey was very good at this by virtue of a combination of personality and push, and a great—if basic—sense of humor. He was seldom at a loss for an answer and was particularly good at handling large crowd scenes. His extrovert nature suited that perfectly.

His social behavior was something else. Bluey liked a drink and had a great capacity for it. In his time he must have virtually bought half a dozen public houses in the West End of London. He was especially popular with the landlord of a well-frequented film and theatre bar, "The Star" in Belgravia, one Paddy Kennedy. Kennedy's forte was insulting people. Bluey would often take well-known international actors with whom he was currently working to experience the Kennedy treatment. Paddy was not impressed by the status of these people and could be quite outrageous. Actors of the ilk of Bob Mitchum and Gregory Peck thought it highly amusing.

Given Bluey's ability to cope with large crowd scenes, the opposite would often apply when he was on a movie with no crowd scenes and a small cast. The relative inaction seemed to bore him. *Zarak*, an action tale made in the part of Morocco that was then Spanish, showed both sides. It involved a large battle scene with the Spanish foreign legion.

The weather had been appalling and the battlefield reduced to a quagmire. Bluey spent two days organizing a full-scale charge. We had four cameras covering this, two of them on a small hill overlooking the battefield.

At last, all was ready. The foreign legion was poised half a mile away or so, and we prepared to roll the cameras. At that precise moment two small dogs appeared directly in front of the cameras and commenced copulating. The legion had been cued to start their charge. In front of the cameras was Bluey, running around in circles, waving his hat and shouting at the dogs. Terence Young, the director, was leaping up and down in exasperation while the unit cheered Bluey on.

By now the legion was well under way, but their ancient and poorly maintained girths and ancillary equipment were snapping and depositing the riders in the mud. By the time the survivors reached the cameras there were only a couple of dozen left, hardly the horde that was required. The whole thing had to be set up again for the following day. Bluey's only comment was that it would have been all right if it hadn't been for "those fucking dogs!" The next day every dog for miles around was rounded up and kept well away from the action. Measures had also been taken to ensure that we had no repeat of, as he put it, "a field full of bedsheets!" This time it was very successful, but the director seemed to think that the original failure was all Bluey's fault.

We returned to England to shoot the interiors at MGM studios, mainly working on small sets with just two or three actors at a time. Terence Young was obviously still harboring suspicions of his assistant director and was looking for an opportunity to catch him out. His chance came one morning when Bluey was half an hour late arriving on the set.

The heroine of *Zarak* was an amply endowed lady, Anita Ekberg, who was on call that morning. Bluey arrived in no great fluster and Terence approached to remonstrate. Bluey had obviously anticipated this, and before Terence could speak he said, "Sorry about the holdup, Guv'nor. I've just been pumping up Ekberg's tits!" Even Terence had to smile at this, and Bluey got away with it.

After that I did not meet up with him again for some years, until a Jerry Lewis–Sammy Davis production, *One More Time*. He was the location manager on this, and as such appeared on the set infrequently— so infrequently that the producer asked Jerry who he was. Jerry, who had often observed Bluey in action at the bar, said that he wasn't certain but he thought that he was a test pilot for Booth's Gin.

Later in his career he managed to acquire the film rights for the *The Rolls Royce Story* and had obtained a certain amount of front money from Cubby Broccoli to develop it. What exactly happened has never been very clear, but it appeared that he continued his campaign to take over certain West End public houses. In consequence he became bankrupt and spent the day prior to the official declaration rushing round his old haunts and depositing his personal effects with the various landlords. Even this did not seem to unduly faze him, and he appeared to carry on more or less as usual.

Sadly, in his declining years he became blind and virtually destitute, but many old friends, including Cubby, remembering him in his glory days, came to the rescue.

Bluey was a character and a half.

# CHAPTER 7

# Africa

In 1953 CinemaScope was being introduced as Twentieth Century Fox's answer to television. Columbia Pictures had plans for some African epics of the great outdoors. What was needed fairly quickly was to amass a variety of library material in the new format, as none existed.

I was dispatched along with three camera crews to photograph landscapes, tribes, the animals, and many other aspects of what was then British East Africa. The Mau Mau insurgency was in full swing. We arrived in Nairobi having traveled via Rome, Cairo, Khartoum, and Entebbe in a piston-engined Argonaut of British Overseas Airways that took some fourteen hours to make the journey. Travel-lagged and slightly deafened, we were booked in to the Lincoln Hotel, which stood among trees in a quiet part of the town. After a meal we were soon in bed.

I was awakened by what sounded like gunfire, near at hand. Thoughts of the Mau Mau sprang to mind. It continued for some three or four minutes, and my imagination rehearsed how to react if an armed insurgent came round the door. Fortunately the sounds became more distant and eventually stopped altogether. I went back to bed but slept only fitfully. The following morning none of the crew had heard anything, most of them saying that they had slept deeply after the journey.

I enquired of the hotel management but they professed to have heard nothing either. Perhaps they did not want to alarm their guests. I was sure that I did not imagine it, and it made for a slightly apprehensive introduction to Africa.

We were due to go through an area up country that had tsetse fly and were duly sent along to a local doctor, one Guy Johnson. The inoculation was made in to the left buttock by a syringe that looked as if it was meant for a horse.

The next day was spent organizing our equipment, transport, and ourselves, before setting off with our White Hunter guides in attendance. We soon ran out of tarmac and proceeded along bumpy dirt roads that didn't do our newly acquired tsetse fly injection areas a lot of good. The fifty-mile journey to our first camp at Maralal was fascinating. The entire terrain was something that none of us had experienced before. Occasionally we'd meet a truck coming from the other way that enveloped us in a cloud of dust. It was our first taste of African dust, which seems to penetrate everywhere. We had plenty more to come

The next two weeks we photographed the mountains and adjacent scenery. The cameras were Arriflex models 2b and 2c. They had been adapted for CinemasScope but were still reasonably light and adaptable. These first two weeks gave us a chance to "road test" the equipment and make any necessary adjustments. The holiday season was soon upon us and, although Maralal was quite high and therefore not too hot, none of us had ever spent a Christmas in a warm climate before. We celebrated in the traditional fashion, the necessary festive food and drink having been sent up to us. The following day we photographed some dancing performed by the local Turkhana tribe. They were obviously not known for the quality of their personal hygiene, and most of the time we were downwind of them, which did not improve our hangovers. It seemed to last a very long time and we were very relieved when at last it was all over.

We had only one day at Maralal, attempting to photograph some animals. The local natives had told our hunters that rhinoceros were around, so we lined the cameras up at the edge of a large wood while native beaters were employed to supposedly drive the beasts toward us. We heard them crashing through the grass and trees, and then suddenly a voice called out, "Here comes one! Turn over!" We promptly did, a little apprehensively, as rhinos were large animals. We saw nothing at first but kept the cameras running. Suddenly a small tusked animal rushed by us. It was a warthog. One of the camera crew, Ernie Day, had given the alarm. After that every warthog was referred to as a Day's Rhino.

I didn't actually see a proper rhino until some six weeks later. The cameraman, Cese Cooney, and I set off early one morning with one of our hunters, who soon picked up a trail. "He's somewhere ahead of us. Go quietly and carefully."

Sure enough, in the trees some two hundred yards away was a large male. We crept along a parallel track one hundred yards from him until we were in front and circled round directly in his path. I set up the camera and we waited. John Lawrence, the hunter, stood right behind me with his rifle leveled. "Don't move and keep quiet!" he murmured. "I won't shoot unless I absolutely have to."

The rhino hove slowly into view, pausing to bite off eucalyptus leaves, to which they are apparently partial. We were rooted to the spot. He was only some thirty yards away. Having digested a mouthful, he turned his head slowly and looked straight at us. His reaction was almost human. He peered hard, scratched himself, and peered again. Subsequently I was told that they are very short-sighted and his actions were like someone reaching for his spectacles. I tried to stop breathing. He ambled forward a few feet, stopped and peered once more.

The tension was unbearable. Then he put his head down and charged. I was "pulling focus" on both the lenses and fumbling with the camera switch, but managed to switch on. At a point when apparently his head was filling the screen and Cese was wondering how long to hold on, he shot off into the bushes. We still kept perfectly still until he had crashed out of sight and sound. John Lawrence said that he was just about to pull the trigger and thought that the rhino was not sure what he was charging and had decided not to risk it. We were all very thankful he did. Months later we saw the shot on screen. It was worth all the nerves and weight loss, and of course, we were now the "rhino experts."

From there we moved up country to Archers Post, which was no more than a large water hole, twenty by sixteen feet, that had been blasted out of the rock by South African engineers during the war, and a few trees. The tents were pitched under them for shade. This area was much lower and therefore hotter. In the morning the sun would appear, a fiery ball on the horizon, and you knew that in an hour or so the temperature would be soaring. However, because we were virtually on the equator, the sun shot up to its zenith very early and descended just as quickly; by 5:30 P.M. it was cool again.

The water hole was a godsend to us. It was full of clear, fresh, running water and wonderful to dive into at the end of the day's work and remove all the dust and grime.

Every week or so an airplane from Nairobi would arrive, bringing mail and important supplies such as beer and gin. The pilot of the plane was a mad Pole who delighted in "shooting up" our camp, raising clouds of dust and blowing everything that was not tied down in all directions. He thought this hysterically funny and refused to desist when asked. He said it created a diversion so we wouldn't get bored.

Bored was the last thing we were. By now we had split up into three groups, shooting in separate areas. At one stage we had one crew in Uganda, one in (then) Tanganyika, and a third nearly up to the Abyssinian border. An edict had arrived from London that wherever possible or feasible we should use "doubles" in the shot. As it was not known at this point which actors would be in what film, this did present a problem. The solution was that we all appeared at intervals as various "names." I, for example, being the shortest of the crew, was Mickey Rooney. Our tall associate producer was Gary Cooper . . . and so on. Neither appeared in the subsequent movie, but you never knew. The feminine side had also not been forgotten. We already had one lady with us, Eva Monley, who was a native of Kenya and spoke Swahili, the lingua franca of East Africa. However, having only one lady to double was not enough, and in any case she was far too busy to spare much time with the shooting unit. So she called up a friend, Maureen Connell, who had acting experience from Nairobi. When she wasn't doubling for Elizabeth Taylor, Katharine Hepburn, Janet Leigh, et al., she worked with the crew and was generally very helpful. Maureen handled this bunch of men, far from home, splendidly and later provided some comic relief.

We were assigned to go down to the famed Serengeti National Park in Tanganikya (or Tanzania, as it now is). As we were in the northern part of Kenya, this meant quite a long journey with a few overnight stops. Heading back toward Nairobi, we stopped for refreshment at the M'Wingo Hotel, right on the equator, which was partly owned by the actor, Bill Holden. Despite the fact we all looked like Ben Gunn with long disheveled hair and a deep tan and were covered with dust, the hotel staff was not concerned. However, a clean-up and a cool beer on the verandah, followed by a cold lunch before we were back on the road again swallowing dust in the accustomed manner, made a pleasant diversion.

Just outside Nairobi are the Aberdare Mountains leading up to the Kinninkop, where Kenyan coffee is grown. As we climbed higher, the air became refreshingly cooler, much to our relief. The purpose of our visit was to get some panoramic shots of the plains and the infinity of Africa. We camped on a football pitch on the edge of a native village and set up camp. As we sat down to eat, we heard the unmistakable sounds of gunfire from the forest above us. A Jeep drove in, quickly spraying dust over our food, and an army officer leapt out.

"Heard you were here," he announced. "Thought I would reassure you that there is nothing to worry about. Just a light skirmish with the Mau Mau. Shouldn't last long, and they are heading away from you." We offered him a beer, but he refused and shot off in another cloud of dust. I don't think anyone slept well that night, as we could still hear the gunfire, albeit getting fainter. We took a very light breakfast and went back down the mountain, grabbing a few shots on the way. The air of slight nervous panic abated as we hit the main road, but we did not linger.

We cut around Nairobi and across the Tanganyika border to the small town of Arusha underneath the cloud-covered peak of Mount Kilimanjaro. A night stop there, then we set off for the Ngorongoro Crater.

The Serengeti Plain is really dead flat here, the heat haze distorting everything as we drove over potholes and large lumps of earth. As we were in convoy with a headwind, the last truck received the majority of the dust. Through this we saw the wildlife. Packs of zebra and antelopes, wildebeest with their large shaggy heads, and lions, some asleep in the heat on their backs with their feet in the air but the lioness ever alert. In the distance among the trees, elephants moved slowly, eating vegetation as they went. Occasionally smaller animals like warthog and the beautiful little civet cat would scatter away as we approached. Even the sight of Africa's "sanitary squad," the mangy hyenas and the scruffy, evil-looking king vultures on the roadside, finishing off the remains of a carcass left by the lions, fascinated us.

We stayed at a conservation lodge from which we had a superb view of the famed crater, which has often been described as the Eighth Wonder of the World. The large Lake Makat lies in its center, and through binoculars we could see hippos, flamingoes, and the sacred ibis on the water's edge. The crater floor itself teemed with wildlife. Sadly, we had no time to really explore this amazing place. As the daylight faded from our lofty viewpoint and infinite Africa slowly disappeared, we went to bed warmly wrapped in blankets for a change, as the night was very cold after what we had been used to.

Because there was so much to photograph during the course of our travels from Archers Post and we had run ourselves short of film—the beautiful fleeting sunrises and sunsets being particularly attractive—we had to await the arrival of our mad Polish flier with a fresh supply sent down from Nairobi. He had been due to meet us here at the crater but so far had not appeared.

There had been a light shower of rain during the night, and next morning I jumped into the Jeep driven by one of our hunters, Bunny Cook, as a change from rattling about in the safari truck. Driving through a thickly treed area with the vegetation dripping, Bunny suddenly stopped the vehicle. "Keep quiet and don't move," he breathed. At first I could see nothing, but Bunny's keen and trained eyes had spotted the large squat animal which was slowly emerging from the bush. It was a Cape buffalo and a very large one. Once before in Archers Post we had gone out to find buffalo but had not found any. On viewing this beast, I was quite pleased that we hadn't. It glared at us with bloodshot eyes, its large head moving from side to side.

Other than an elephant, it was the biggest animal I had ever seen. Its black skin was steaming. We sat tight. From the corner of my eye I saw Bunny's arm slowly reach down for the rifle by his side. The buffalo lowered its head and took a step forward, continuing to watch us. After what seemed an eternity, it turned and ambled off in to the bush.

"Phew," said Bunny, "That was too close for comfort. I really thought that he was going to charge us. I'm rather glad he didn't." He drove off quickly, explaining that buffalo were extremely difficult to shoot; their skin is like armor plate. He personally had once put eight rounds of heavy-caliber bullets into one and it still kept coming on as he fled in his Jeep. When wounded, apparently, they would hunt you. "So you see what I mean," he chuckled. I certainly did.

Well, this was the Africa I had wanted to see, and I was certainly getting my money's worth, I thought. We traveled on, Bunny sensibly keeping in front of the convoy to escape the all-enveloping dust blowing back onto us. We had come down from the escarpment and were bouncing across flat countryside. Suddenly there was a roar of aircraft engine and the airplane piloted by our Polish friend had arrived. It went ahead, described a slow turn and came back toward us. As it did we saw a bright object on a small flag drop out. We drew up to where the object lay to find it was a metal film can. Inside was a note: "Mail dropped approximately 1 mile up road." This was received with great interest, as we had had none for three weeks.

But what was meant by "up the road?" Did he mean back up from where we were, or a mile farther on? By this time we had been traveling for some four hours and none of us felt like retracing our steps. Anyway, he must mean farther on, mustn't he? So we proceeded slowly, everyone peering to each side of the truck, and stopped at intervals while we all got out and prowled around. Nothing, but we kept looking. Eventually, some hours later, the can was found. It contained ten letters in all. Nine of them were for the cameraman, John Wilcox, and one for me. It was a bank statement.

Some two hours later we arrived at the Masai village of Lolliondo on the Kenyan border. The Masai are quite a unique tribe in African terms, unusually tall and brown rather than black, as they were of Coptic origin from the far north. They are extremely well organized within themselves and their social and moral structure is very rigid. We were told that they believed that they owned all the cattle in the world. They had large herds that sustained them and they used them for barter and sometimes currency.

On arrival we met the incumbent District Officer, who looked like Rex Harrison and sported a turban. A large Rhodesian Ridgeback dog accompanied him. Obviously white company was infrequent and he was delighted to see us. Over dinner (roast guinea fowl) he regaled us with fascinating stories of the Masai and his long term of office in Africa. He did appear to be a trifle eccentric which, I suppose, was not surprising in light of his circumstances.

On reaching a certain age and in order to prove their manhood, the young Masai men have to go through certain initiation ceremonies. One of them was to hunt lion armed with only a spear and a short stabbing knife. He must not return until he had killed the lion. We were to photograph this event. Early next morning the youth set off, with us following with the Jeep and the camera. Around his knees he wore small bells, which jangled loudly. This was extremely useful to us as he ran very quickly, diving in and around bushes, sometimes only the bells telling us where he was. We were bouncing and crashing over the rough country and finding it difficult to keep up with him.

After an hour or so he stopped and indicated that he was taking a short rest. Gratefully we climbed out of the Jeep to smooth out our aches and pains. In no time at all he was off again, while we piled into the Jeep in pursuit. Shortly he disappeared altogether into a heavily wooded area and we heard a cry and a lion's roar. He obviously was a very efficient hunter; by the time we found him the lion was lying dead at his feet. And we had not managed to actually photograph the kill.

Nevertheless, by setting up some shots we did cobble together a convincing sequence. The lion was loaded on to the Jeep, but the young warrior declined the offer of a lift, as that sort of behavior was frowned upon.

Back in the village the evening was spent watching the Masai giving an initiation party for the young man, complete with dance. This consisted of a long line circling the campfire and performing prodigious leaps in to the air, each dancer striving to outdo the others. Having had a few celebratory drinks ourselves, John Wilcox and I got onto the end of the line. Fortunately the Masai found this amusing. Coming down from an airborne leap John landed awkwardly on his ankle, and I had to assist him back to his room in the D.C's bungalow. The Masai thought that this was even more amusing.

Our bedroom in the bungalow was open at both ends, with a bed on either side of a narrow passage. Fatigued by the day's affairs, I soon dropped off to sleep, only to be awakened by a loud noise that sounded like someone sawing through a rusty nail. It gradually receded into the distance. I mentioned this to the D.C. the next morning. "Oh, yes," he said casually "That's fairly common here."

"What is?"

"Oh, don't worry. It sounds like a leopard passing through. They're nocturnal, you know." I made quite sure that the bedroom entrances were boarded up that night.

The following morning was leopard morning. Leopards will kill at night and hang the carcass on a strong tree branch out of the reach of scavengers and let it rot for a few days, before returning to eat it. They don't like their food fresh. Bunny Cook, our hunter, had spotted a gazelle carcass in a tree a few miles away, so we set off at dawn. We were given to understand that leopards like to breakfast early.

Bumping over extremely rough ground covered in thick grass, we suddenly dropped into a deep hole, the steering wheel driving hard into Bunny's stomach. He coughed and groaned, his sunburnt face getting paler and a trickle of blood appearing from the side of his mouth. Clearly something was seriously wrong. We pulled him from the driving cab, laid him down on the sorbo-rubber sheets we used for the camera equipment, and drove slowly back to the camp. He managed to tell us he had an ulcer, which must have burst on contact with the steering wheel. He was obviously a hospital case. Fortunately just above us in the hills was a small radio station and after some delay an aircraft arrived from Nairobi.

Somebody had to go with Bunny to attend to him on the flight, and after some discussion I was selected. We took off from the tiny landing strip at Lolliondo in a light Comanche aircraft while I acted as nurse to Bunny, who was still losing blood. The journey took barely forty minutes, but I was profoundly relieved to land and get Bunny to hospital.

Eva Monley and our production manager, Andy Worker, were there to meet us, and after getting Bunny into an ambulance, they escorted me to the famous New Stanley Hotel.

This was only the second time in three months that I had been in civilization since our arrival, and that was counting our brief stop at the M'Wingo Hotel on our way to the Serengeti. After a bath and shave I thought I would take advantage of this unexpected situation and have a haircut in the hotel's barber shop. It was as well I was not charged for the time taken to remove my long flowing locks, for it took quite a while. I felt positively nude afterwards.

Andy had suggested that I come out with him and a few Nairobi people for dinner and a look at the sights. After living from the "pot" for the last few weeks, this was indeed manna. Off we went to the Equator Club for a few drinks and a little entertainment. I was thoroughly enjoying the unexpected novelty of all this; it was like being taken on a special outing for being a good boy. I was informed by my companions that this was a special cabaret night to be enlivened by the appearance of a striptease artist with the unlikely name of Fifi La Bonbon.

We were a merry crowd with much to talk about, and Andy told me that he had had a cable from London that morning to say that they were pleased with our current batch of "dailies." The drink had been flowing freely and I realized that it was about time I bought a round and looked round for a steward to place an order. There were none in sight. The manager to whom I had been introduced was nearby, and I asked him where they all were.

With a completely straight face and in true Colonial manner he informed that the Africans were not allowed to be present "while the *memsahib* doffs her kit." That made my evening, and I have dined out on that story on several occasions.

As it turned out, the Africans did not miss a lot, as Miss La Bonbon would not have made it at The Crazy Horse in Paris. A very C3 desultory sort of performance it was, but what with coming in from the wilds and the demon drink, I applauded and cheered wildly.

We eventually wound up a most enjoyable evening and I went back to the New Stanley. Eva had told me that they were trying to get a replacement hunter, but it was unlikely that one would be found until midday tomorrow. I sank into the luxury of a proper bed, and within minutes the phone rang. It was Eva to tell me that they had found one, but he had to be fetched from a town called Eldoret, which was up north, and I was to be ready to take off at dawn. So much for a good night's sleep.

Arriving at the airport bleary-eyed and not a little hungover, we boarded the plane. Even my delicate condition could not keep me from appreciating the superb spectacle of the African dawn. It was truly magnificent, the colors constantly changing as it got lighter. An hour's fly-ing took us to Eldoret, where we picked up David Noonan. David was everyone's conception of a White Hunter. Tall, slim, and good-looking, he said very little and smoked an occasional pipe. I subsequently spent a lot of time with him and found him to be a very interesting compan-ion.

By the time we commenced our journey back to Lolliondo it was ap-proaching midday and our flight path took us over the Great Rift Val-ley, a vast natural fault which stretched over a few thousand miles. It was the worst possible time to fly over such a place, the heat creating air thermals that caused the light aircraft to drop, climb, and bounce in the ensuing turbulence. It was not a sensation I enjoyed even in the best of health, but in my hungover and sleepless condition I began to feel a little uncharacteristically airsick.

It was with great relief that we finally cleared the Rift and the plane settled down. As we approached the airstrip we saw that it was covered with animals, as was normal. The usual technique was to fly low over them until they dispersed and gave us space to land. Whether he had realized my fragile state and therefore thought it would be amusing, I know not, but the pilot made a meal again out of this maneuver, fin-ishing up by climbing steeply upwards almost to stalling point and then dropping straight down in a sort of negative "G" force. He was a mar-velous pilot, but I was in no condition to appreciate his expertise. Ap-parently I emerged from the plane a peculiar facial mixture of brown, white, and green. I received no sympathy from my colleagues when they discovered the cause.

The rest of the Lolliondo trip passed without further incident, so we said goodbye to the courteous Masai, having paid them for their ser-vices by the unique method of purchasing some of their cattle, using the D.C. as an intermediary, and then handing them back to them. Ap-parently the money was kept in a special fund for the Masais' general welfare. It seemed to me that somehow we had come out on the wrong side of the bargain, but we had what we had come for, and all honor was satisfied.

We went back to Archers Post to wait for the rest of the crew to re-assemble. We had nothing specific to photograph, so we spent the time looking for elephant, of which we had seen signs. Sitting on top of the safari truck by a dried-up riverbed, I witnessed a family approaching the far bank, two adults and two small young ones. Father Jumbo slid down the bank and carefully made his way to the other side and scrambled up, then waved his trunk. The two babies came next, carefully putting their feet exactly where Father had, even though they were at full stretch. Mother brought up the rear, and as Father pulled them up by his trunk she shoved them up from behind. They then fell in to line ahead and shambled off. I managed to shoot this delightful sequence and I believe it was subsequently used in a Columbia movie.

We were getting through our now fairly organized schedule in good order, but some further "atmosphere" material was requested by London. We went north toward the Kenya–Ethiopian border.

This time we traveled through country very different from what we were used to. This was desert in the true meaning of the word. From Archers Post to our first stop at Marsubit we saw nothing but sand and a scattering of shrub. Marsubit itself sat on a small hill and was a real oasis, with just a small lodge where we slept. The morning revealed dewy grass, a sight we had not seen since the Aberdares.

Traveling with us was a unit of Askaris (African soldiers) who were to relieve a similar force at our final destination at Northhorr. It was apparently a Beau Geste type of border fort, complete with patrolling camel corps who were defending the Kenyan border from sporadic sorties from the Ethiopian side. What they hoped to gain from this vast arid area I never discovered. To get there from Marsubit we had to traverse the Chalbi Desert—extreme heat, a poor track, and the ubiquitous dust. And just sand, with very distant hills and the occasional mirage. This part of the journey took some three hours, so we were very pleased to reach our destination, such as it was. Fortunately we were to spend only one night there, unlike the camel corps, whose schedule was different from ours; they were not apparently due in the fort for another week.

We were not too dismayed at this, as we had shot some interesting desert material on the way up. We set off at dawn, hoping to make it to Marsubit before it got too hot. Incredibly, there had been a light rainfall overnight, and where yesterday had been unbroken sand there was now a carpet of tiny red and blue flowers. These had appeared in twelve hours. Apparently this was nothing out of the ordinary, being actually a regular occurrence. To us, it was amazing.

Our progress to Marsubit was delayed as the safari truck containing the relieved Askari troops bogged down in the sand and it took the better part of an hour to get it out. The flowers were photographed in great detail while this was going on. By the time we were under way again, the sun was high and the heat excessive, so the distant sight of Marsubit perched on its hill was most welcome.

Back at camp we waited for the other crews to return, as an edict had arrived from London to say that enough African footage had been gathered and we should return home. So it was goodbye to Archers Post and off for a last dusty drive to Nairobi. It had been nearly five months since we had left there, and none of us except me had been near Nairobi since. Naturally the others reacted as I had done and wanted to dive into the fleshpots—such as they were.

In the famous Long Bar at the New Stanley Hotel, we were aware of men wearing guns and women with a firearm in their handbags. Many of these we gathered were farmers from up country, just visiting. They were full of tales of the Mau Mau in their area and the need to be vigilant. I did not envy them their situation.

We enplaned at the beginning of May, and I spent most of the flight before Cairo looking through the observation window at Africa beneath us.

Later that year I made my second trip to Africa, with a full crew and cast, to shoot the location footage for *Safari,* featuring Victor Mature and Janet Leigh. Again we established our base camp back at Archers Post and its pool.

Vic Mature was always a cheerful, ebullient fellow (if a trifle noisy), and Janet warm and friendly. Once again we took our nightly swim to wash away the grime of the day. The pool itself was not more than five feet deep, so after a swim up and down its length or so, it was customary to lean against the bank chatting to whoever happened to be there. I was doing exactly that when Janet happened by and also leaned against the side. After a couple of minutes of idle chatter I suddenly felt a hand "touch me up." Janet smiled sweetly and swam away. Hello! I thought. Could it be that the leading lady fancied me? This vanity was quickly dispelled as I now observed her talking to one of the sound boys on the other side. He suddenly gave a compulsive start and looked hard at Janet as once again she swam away. I hastened across and consulted.

He had had the same experience. What was going on? We both watched as she next joined our assistant director. Again, the same thing. Just then a spluttering Vic Mature surfaced hard by and both he and Janet collapsed with laughter. It had been a put-up job between them.

For a brief moment, a few high hopes had been held!

Remembering Vic Mature brings to mind Elizabeth Taylor. I never actually worked with her, but while shooting *Zarak* in Morocco, also starring Vic, I met her at midnight in the Casbah of the town of Tetuan where we were shooting. After absorbing some local color with some other members of the crew, I was on my way home. Round a corner came Vic with a lady on his arm. They were lost, having just returned from a night in Tangier. I directed them to the hotel, feeling that I had seen that girl somewhere before, but it wasn't until later that I realized who she was.

Liz was not in the picture and was only visiting her then husband, Michael Wilding, who was. She came to the set most days and was always friendly and chatty. In fact she used to mix in with the crew and often did little errands for us. We had a wonderful Cockney grip who was a great character, and he and Liz became great mates. Bert was always getting her to help him in some way or another, and one day when we were fighting the light, the refreshments arrived. Unable to find time to fetch them, Bert said, "'Ere Liz, get the drinks for us, there's a good girl." "OK, Bert," she replied, "how many of them take sugar?"

She became our tea girl from then on.

# CHAPTER 8

∿

# Sea Tales and Adventures

*The Cockleshell Heroes* was a CinemaScope picture for Columbia Pictures under the banner of its subsidiary, Warwick Films. It was to prove more than interesting.

It was the story of the Royal Marine Commando wartime raid on the German submarine base at St. Lazaire in Western France, to be directed by José Ferrer, who also starred in it along with Trevor Howard. It was the only other film that I worked on that had five different directors—*Casino Royale* had six, if I remember rightly.

From the beginning, a certain amount of bad chemistry existed. Ted Moore, the director of photography, and Ferrer did not exactly hit it off, and Joe cordially hated the producer, Irving Allen. This eventually did come to a head. In my experience it is always difficult to both direct and play in a film, as the two functions often conflict, as they did here.

We were shooting in the River Tagus and along the Portuguese coast near Lisbon. Working at sea with action boats is never easy and very time-consuming. We seemed to spend an inordinate amount of time doing close shots of Ferrer to the detriment of Trevor Howard (and the other actors). That did not help relationships with them, or with the producer, for that matter. So we didn't exactly start off too well, and the first two weeks' shooting was a little fraught. Ferrer did not easily take to advice from his senior technicians and became very dogmatic and authoritarian. It didn't help matters that he was often proved wrong.

Relationships with the producer finally broke down at a dailies in a Lisbon cinema. Irving Allen expressed his disapproval at what he was viewing in a very loud voice, with the whole unit present. This was too much for Ferrer. He cursed Irving loudly, leapt over the seats, and left the cinema. They never spoke to each other again. The next day we carried on as usual, Joe still at the helm. It appeared that he had a watertight contract for the whole film and could not be replaced.

Ted Moore's relationship with him was not improved when we shot a "day for night" sequence of one of the canoes hiding under a pier, supposedly in the St. Lazaire harbor. In endeavoring to balance the arc filler light on the actors in the foreground against a blinding white sky, Ted made a miscalculation, and it did not work. It was decided to replace him with the second unit director of photography, John Wilcox.

Things in the camera department became a little easier, but the director's relationship with his actors did not improve. Trevor took great exception to Ferrer's attitude and went missing for a short while in Lisbon. As usual he was found in a bar. He made it generally known that he was far from happy with the whole situation. However, despite all this, we progressed, but came the day when we had to put to sea with the canoes containing the commandos. Not only did we have to deal with the boats themselves but also with navigation, timing, tides and the weather, and all that made for a pretty potent cocktail. Not to mention that one or two of the actors were poor sailors.

Our first seaborne efforts were disastrous, to put it mildly. There was a strong wind blowing and a fast tide running, making the boats very difficult to maneuver. They were all over the place, like rowboats on a boating lake on a weekend. Communications were also difficult because of the wind. All in all, it was a shambles. The final straw came when the leading canoe sprang a bad leak, creating panic among the actors. It was decided to go back to base, regroup, and start again.

A new plan of action was decided upon, but the next day's shooting was aborted because a small gale had sprung up and the seas were running high. We shot some land footage instead. The feedback from the actors was that it all could be shot from the shore. Joe Ferrer was none too pleased with this. He had had quite enough from them as it was.

The next day dawned bright and clear, with virtually no wind, so off we went boating again. This time things went well and, apart from the odd collision and some of the boats suddenly veering off in the wrong direction, we accomplished a fair amount of useful footage, much to the actors'—and everyone else's—relief.

I got the feeling that, if the day had not gone well, we may well have had an actor's rebellion on our hands, such was Joe's cavalier treatment of them. It was generally observed that being an actor himself didn't help all that much. As it was, an uneasy truce prevailed.

Fortunately the better weather continued, and we were able to finish off the seagoing sequences but not without a certain continuing animosity. It was a relief to return to the comparative tranquility of the studio back in England. Here things went much better, but Joe Ferrer's contract expired before we actually finished, something that Irving Allen had been waiting for. When he had gone without saying goodbye to anybody, we had a series of directors, from the assistant director Max Varnel, to the location manager Bluey Hill, the editor Alan Osbiston, and, finally, Irving himself to finish it off.

Contrary to what usually happens when a picture is subjected to a plethora of directors, the end result was well received. But it was not one of my favorite movies to work on.

Some five years later I worked on another epic full of sea sequences—*The Guns of Navarone*. In 1960 it was the biggest picture of the year, costing three million dollars. By today's standards, that's a fairly low budget, but at the time it was considered expensive. It had a star-studded cast consisting of David Niven, Anthony Quinn, Gregory Peck, Stanley Baker, Jimmy Darren, Irene Pappas, and Gia Scala. And it had a shooting schedule of ten months—also considered lavish. It was to be directed by Alexander (Sandy) Mackendrick and to be shot on mainland Greece with the island of Rhodes as Navarone. It had been adapted from a novel by Alistair Maclean. It was also going to be shot in CinemaScope, using the combined lens system I have described elsewhere with all its heavy ancillary equipment.

It had been decided that we do some preproduction shooting for two weeks, mainly for the title sequence and some atmospheric material of the Greek islands. We commenced outside Athens doing long shots of the sea and including a large fleet of naval vessels supplied by the

Greek navy. This had initially presented a problem to the director of photography, Oswald Morris, as it was a night sequence covering a vast expanse of water and obviously had to be shot as "day for night." Ossie disliked the conventional "blue" look of the method traditionally used, and we had experimented with filters normally used for monochrome photography. This filled the processing laboratory, Technicolor, with alarm, but Ossie achieved what he wanted—a much more natural look. It worked splendidly.

For the title sequence a shot of the famous Parthenon at sunrise was wanted, and we went up the preceding day to select a camera position. As it was forbidden to deface this ancient building, we huddled together in a group while someone marked the spot with grease pencil. We arrived before dawn next morning and tried to find the spot. This involved me crawling about on my hands and knees clutching a torch. In the meantime the sky was getting progressively lighter. Finally, as I had never found the exact place, we settled on a position and proceeded to immortalize the magnificent spectacle of the sun appearing through the venerable stone columns. We were only just in time.

After a few more days of this type of material we embarked for Rhodes. Another three days were spent picking up atmospheric material before the main unit and the actors arrived. One morning we toiled away in the hot sun while Sandy endeavored to choose some camera set-ups. He had made copious drawings of the shots required, but wherever we went he did not seem to be satisfied that we were in the right place. By lunchtime we had shot nothing and were a little weary; we had covered a lot of territory, carrying the bulky CinemaScope equipment. Ossie Morris pointed this out to Sandy, who rather reluctantly agreed to shoot a couple of shots.

That evening there was a meeting between Sandy and Carl Foreman, the executive producer, with the result that poor Sandy was fired. Possibly Carl felt that Sandy would not meet the schedule. Whatever the reason, here we were, on the eve of commencing the main shooting, without a director—but we were informed that we would have a new one in the morning.

It was J. Lee Thompson. He had been on holiday in Athens when Carl phoned him and had jumped on a plane immediately. So at last we started shooting the movie proper, with a director who had barely had time to read the script. Lee was a nervous man who "earthed" his nerves by constantly rolling pieces of paper between his fingers. The continuity girl had to have an endless supply of old torn-up call sheets, etc. to hand. His baptism to the movie could not have been more fraught. Here he was, only roughly aware of the script for this epic, and surrounded by some of the biggest names in Hollywood with vast experience among them.

He handled it very well and things proceeded smoothly, the actors accepting him and sympathetic to the fact that he had had it sprung on him at the last moment. And, because of their experience, they were very easy to work with. David Niven, with whom I had worked before, was his usual affable self, as were Gregory Peck and Stan Baker. Anthony Quayle was a trifle nervous.

The oldest hand of them all, Tony Quinn, seldom spoke to anyone and spent most of the time when he was not in the current shot playing chess. When he did speak he was monosyllabic, and when asked to reposition himself for a shot, for example, he just did it with no comment. One certainly got the feeling that he had done it all before, which he certainly had. At the end of the long schedule he departed without a word. I met up with him again on another movie some years later, politely said hello, and reminded him of our previous meeting. He just nodded. I never discovered whether he was arrogant or just shy.

One or two of the locations were on the other side of the island and necessitated long trips over rough country. The equipment—and we had quite a lot of it—was carried on mules. The caravan wound its way slowly over the hard terrain, taking an hour or more to reach its destination. This meant an early rise and departure from the hotel of a morning, setting off and returning in the dark. We were often delayed by having to retrieve mules that had wandered off. They were long, quite arduous days in very hot sun.

We occasionally had some comic relief, which was welcome. The actors obviously knew a thing or two about making movies and seldom missed an opportunity to exploit it. In the nicest professional way they upstaged one another, given the opportunity.

A short sequence required them, disguised in German uniform, to peer over a wall at a German army detachment in the road below. They approached it slowly and carefully, looked over, and backed slowly away. The camera was shooting slightly up at them, so they gradually disappeared as they retreated. Years of Hollywood experience had taught them to keep their face in shot as long as possible only just turning away before they disappeared. Even then it was hard work convincing Messrs. Niven, Peck, and Quinn not to steal a last look to the front. They just did it automatically. On this occasion it did look a little comic on the screen, so we re-shot it, this time with them turning away earlier and not looking back.

Greg Peck had this down to a fine art. When a reaction was called for, or requiring him to look round, he took his time about it. We calculated that it usually took him fully half a minute (45 to 50 feet of film) to execute it, guaranteeing him maximum screen time.

Given the conditions, things had gone well. We had finished at the more remote locations and were now working much closer to our base at the hotel. One sequence contained a Greek wedding, complete with their famous dancing and plate throwing. This developed into a slight farce. The plates were supposedly thrown in by the cast and bit players, but it got a trifle out of hand as the unit joined in and the air was thick with flying plates. While the unit enjoyed it, Lee Thompson was not amused, as a plate struck him on the ear. They were only made of plaster, but he expressed himself forcibly. The situation deteriorated further as we all had a severe attack of the giggles and were glared at accordingly. He obviously had a short fuse.

But we were on schedule, and Carl Foreman was very happy with the footage to date. We had the usual flying visits from the Columbia hierarchy, ostensibly to see that all was well but in fact a "freebie" trip and a short holiday at the company's expense. They were frequently to be seen—at least for the first day—in earnest consultation with either Carl or Lee, no doubt discussing the movie in general. Having done their duty, they disappeared and were only seen again some days later passing through the hotel foyer with their bags, en route to the airport.

We duly took to sea to film a sequence of the boat containing our heroes on its way to Navarone. The boat was a flat-bottomed Greek fishing boat called a caïque. It had virtually no keel, and even in slight sea conditions would roll quite alarmingly. Its one-stroke engine meant it could proceed only slowly.

We managed to pack quite a few people aboard. There is a long shot in the finished picture taken from one end of the boat showing the full length of it. No one would suspect that not a few members of the unit were hanging over the side only just out of picture.

The first day could hardly be called an unqualified success. Maneuvering the caïque was ponderous and took time. The first time we had everything right and the sun in the right place, we turned over just as the catering boat steamed leisurely through the frame. Some harsh comments on its navigational capabilities resounded before we could go again. We had been towing behind us a boat carrying the generator that was driving the two large Brute arc lights we had on board the caïque. The connecting cables stretched across the gap between us and parted just as we turned over for the second time. We tried again.

Then the wind sprang up. One of the characteristics of the Mediterranean is that a storm will blow up very quickly and with virtually no warning, and just as quickly subside. The wind strengthened and the rain sheeted down. We took what little cover there was. The sea had developed long deep waves, and the flat-bottomed caïque began to roll badly, everyone hanging on to any loose equipment. Further shooting being clearly impossible, we headed for the harbor, once straddled by one of the Seven Wonders of the World, the Colossus of Rhodes.

The next day the sea was like a millpond, which is typical of the Mediterranean, and with no further interruptions of any sort, we shot the entire sequence. That completed, we continued shooting on dry land, leaving any further sea material to the second unit, as none of it required the main actors.

Back to the action: Our heroes finally make it up to the gun emplacement where they have to destroy the guns. They eliminate the guards and charge everything with dynamite, leaving only the fuse to be lit. Everyone else departs, leaving Greg Peck to do it. After the ignition he dives off the platform some one hundred feet into the sea.

Bob Simmons, the stuntman who was to execute the dive, spent some time choosing the right location. The place he eventually selected was a sheer drop into the sea surrounded by some protruding rocks. It was extremely dangerous. He actually did it twice, skillfully avoiding the rocks. On the screen the result was spectacular. Bob really did earn his money that day.

The main unit shooting on Rhodes was completed straightforwardly enough, so we left the second unit behind to finish everything off and returned to England and the studio to complete the ten-month-long schedule. The sinking of the caïque and the beginning of the climb up the sheer cliffs were shot in the large tank on "H" stage at Shepperton Studios. The faultless matching with the actual exteriors convinced many people that the entire sequence had been done on Rhodes.

The picture became a great success and fully justified all the planning and hard work that had gone into it. As opposed to *Cockleshells*, we had had no problems with actors or the director.

It was a long, tough movie to make—but an enjoyable one.

# CHAPTER 9

~

# Travels with Joe

In 1957 we set off for Saigon (as it was then called) to make *The Quiet American*, based on a Graham Greene novel. The crew was international, consisting of a mixture of English, American, Italian, along with a few French and the local Vietnamese. The trip out, a long and arduous one, was in an Air France piston-engined Constellation and took some thirty-six hours. We seemed to come down everywhere for fuel, and the trip was interminable. By the time we eventually arrived we were half deaf from the engine noise and suffering extreme piston-engine lag.

The time was just after the French Indo-Chinese war; the French had gone but had left their architectural legacy. The city was known as the Paris of the East, and it was easy to understand why. The wide tree-lined streets and the buildings were pure France. The cuisine, however, was something else again, as we were to discover.

The director was Joseph L. Mankiewicz, who had also written the screenplay, and the main cast consisted of Audie Murphy, Michael Redgrave, and an Italian actress, Georgia Moll. Graham Greene had been out there some years before, and the story was supposedly based on his own experiences.

Joe Mankiewicz had brought with him a production manager, an art director, an editor, Billy Hornbeck, and two special-effects experts named Rocky and George. This duo would provide extremely good value as the film progressed. They arrived in great style in their own Dakota aircraft, complete with built-in workshop. It soon became obvious that they were a law unto themselves and would brook no interference from anyone.

The picture was to be made in monochrome. The original conception was to have it tinted in sepia, to get the warmth of the Orient and the local faces, etc. but it was eventually abandoned because each print had to be dyed individually and a series of tests proved that there was no consistency from print to print.

The camera and sound crews, continuity girl, and makeup and hairdressing experts were English. While American crews tended to address one another with "Mr." and "Sir," after a suitable period English crews usually used given names. This was perfectly acceptable to Joe Mankiewicz, who seemed to enjoy the novelty of it, but not his production manager, who informed us that he had worked with Joe for twenty years and had never called him by his Christian name. We simply asked him why not and carried on as usual. He never did call Mankiewicz "Joe," and he obviously harbored the thought that we were disrespectful, not to say insolent. But it certainly didn't bother Joe and throughout the movie we enjoyed a marvelous working relationship with him. He was very appreciative and a delight to work with.

After three weeks of shooting that had gone well, we moved farther north to a small town called Tay Ninh. During the recent war with France, Tay Ninh had been the headquarters of a gentleman named General Thé, who commanded a very large independent army of his own. According to local information, he fought on the side that he considered to be currently winning, obviously thinking that this was diplomacy of the highest order.

The reason that he possessed this army was that Tay Ninh was the capital and Holy See of a unique religious cult called the Cao Dai, which had two million adherents, and he felt that in view of this he should have a large say as to who was going to be running the country.

The cult was based on a curious mixture of Buddhism, Catholicism, Confucianism, and Taoism. Its patron saints were Victor Hugo, Sun Yat Sen, Jean-Paul Sartre, and a Vietnamese poet named Nguyen Binh Khiem. Above the altar were paintings of Buddha, Jesus Christ, Confucius, and a Taoist leader. We were informed by a public relations representative that Joan of Arc had been in touch in 1926 and that they were expecting to hear from Shakespeare at any time.

Its temple had a Gothic–cum–Walt Disney appearance, with marble snakes coiled around Doric columns, gold everywhere, and above it all a huge eye gazing down. This, we were told, was the Eye of the All-seeing God. The ceiling was mainly a large open grid from which came the sound of chains being dragged across. This, we understood, was to symbolize purgatory. The whole place had a very unnerving atmosphere. The sound crew had to spend a night there recording tracks, an experience they admitted they could have done without.

We were told that it was very fortuitous that we had arrived on that particular day, as they were having a special celebration that included a procession we might wish to photograph. This was not of value to the film, but somebody thought that it would be good public relations if we did so.

It was a very colorful affair. All the cardinals, many of whom were women, were clad in flowing robes of many bright hues. They carried large banners written in Vietnamese, and it wasn't until it was all over that one of our interpreters told us that they were anti-government slogans. This was to produce a slight problem later on. There had been no word from Shakespeare when we left.

We carried on in Saigon mainly in the streets and in the slightly less salubrious Chinese quarter of Cholon, constantly surrounded by a large crowd. Cholon possessed a unique establishment called the Tour D'Ivoire (The Ivory Tower), which consisted of a cocktail bar on the first floor, a restaurant on the second, and a dance floor on the third. We shot a sequence there with Redgrave and Murphy. Joe Mankiewicz had been told by the manager that at certain times the dance hall exhibited what was rather coyly known as a *tableau vivante*. He thought that this might provide a good background to a further dialogue between them and inquired as to when we could shoot there. The exact nature of the *tableau vivante* was left to the imagination, but I think that the manager had second thoughts about having it actually photographed. When told that our schedule could fit in at certain times, he always explained that the performers were either on holiday or, on one occasion, had gone to supper at the time we required them. The idea was eventually abandoned, much, I think, to the manager's relief, even allowing for the money he would have made out of it.

Years later I mentioned this to Sandy Gall, who was by then a TV news presenter but had spent some time in Saigon as a Reuters correspondent. He remembered the *tableau vivante* well, as it was apparently raided regularly by the local police, it being a bit too much even for them. So it was probably just as well that we never photographed it.

Then a problem arose with reference to our trip to Tay Ninh to photograph the Cao Dai sect. We had run out of time and had been unable to complete the sequence there; permission to return had been requested. By this time the government had been made aware of the "anti" slogans inscribed on the parade banners and demanded the return of the film. After some tricky negotiations most of the material was returned, but we were categorically refused permission to revisit the town.

This was not good enough for Audie Murphy, America's most decorated soldier, and he volunteered to lead us back, brandishing his service revolver. Fortunately the offer was tactfully declined. In the end we mocked up a section of the temple in the Rome studio to get the required footage.

One of the highlights of the picture was to be the blowing up of a large square right in the middle of Saigon. This was where Rocky and George came into their own. Having littered the square with old cars and various other items of detritus, they set to work with a will. Starting at dawn, which was around 6:00 A.M., they systematically rigged the square with explosives everywhere.

Mankiewicz was anxious to start shooting, because the preparation was taking a little longer than he thought, but the special effects duo would not be hurried. It would be ready when they said it was. Eventually they condescended to imply that it would be ready by lunchtime, and at noon we had all the cameras in position and ready to roll. Mankiewicz looked around to ascertain exactly where the explosions would be and when. Rocky and George were not to be seen. It turned out that they had gone to lunch, not having had a break for some seven hours.

They returned promptly at 2:00 P.M., ignoring any remonstration or witty remarks, and blew up the square. It was quite sensational. Everything happened exactly as they had said it would. After the smoke cleared away, Joe said, "Thanks, boys, that was great." Rocky and George just nodded and disappeared, and were not seen again for some days. They were phlegmatic, to put it mildly.

Although it was customary when on location to shoot a six-day week and have the Sunday as a rest day, we found ourselves with one whole weekend free due to a shift in the schedule and the nonavailability of one of the locations. With nothing left to fill in the time, we planned to form a group and fly to Cambodia and visit the historic site and ancient city of Angkor Wat. Air Vietnam in those days boasted only two aircraft, one Dakota (DC-3) and a DC-4. We were advised to take the DC-4, which was reasonably new and flown by a Frenchman. So we duly assembled at the airport, only to find that the DC-4 was not available; the pilot was suffering from an attack of piles and could not fly. So the Dakota it was.

The one-and-a-half-hour flight was very noisy, but most of the time we spent filling in forms for the Cambodian Immigration and Customs. One of them said "Occupation." In a fit of whimsy I put "Sagger Makers Bottom Knocker." Naturally all the rest had sensibly entered "Film Technician."

All went well until we got to Immigration at the Siam Rap airport. The officials wanted to know (a) What did my profession actually mean? And (b) Why was I the only one among all these film technicians? So much for trying to be amusing. This held up the others in the airport while I endeavored to talk my way out of that one. I was not over popular by the time I joined them on the airport coach.

The coach itself was a splendid thing. Well stricken in years, it had a "bar" in the front consisting of a number of bottles containing various colored liquids with a thick horde of flies all over them. We abstained from quenching our thirst. The coach also appeared to have no suspension whatsoever, so we rattled and bounced along the rocky dirt road, which was full of potholes. And so to Angkor Wat.

I will not try to describe it, as it has been well documented by others, but it was something I will always remember. Reclaimed from the jungle and in amazing condition for its believed age, it amazed us with its incredible craftsmanship and detail. We wandered about at will, inspecting, discussing, and photographing and occasionally catching a glimpse of our leading man, Michael Redgrave, refreshing himself from a bottle of gin behind one of the walls.

After three hours or so we repaired, hot and thirsty, to the hotel for refreshment and returned to the airport aboard the ancient coach. The Dakota was there but not the pilot. It was explained that he had gone to visit some friends but would be back any minute. He eventually returned some two hours later, having, he said, broken down in the taxi. At least we could appreciate that, since the taxi was probably of the same vintage as the airport coach.

I managed to resist the temptation to be witty on the Vietnam immigration forms as we returned to Saigon.

A week later we finished shooting in Saigon and prepared to fly to Rome to shoot the interiors in Cinecitta studios. Because we were a very large crew, it was decided to dispatch us on three separate flights. I was booked on the last to leave, accompanying the camera equipment, which of course was very heavy. At the last minute it was found that the entire crew of a Chinese merchant ship were on the same plane, flying back to take another ship. The question of the overall weight on the aircraft now arose. So every one of the sailors was individually weighed, along with their luggage, and I think four of them were eventually put off, to answer the problem.

I arrived in Rome and found a pleasant flat near the Borghese Park, then we started in the studio. This initially had problems for the sound department. Cinecitta was sited near the then main Rome airport at Ciampino, and the large aircraft roared directly over the studio. For Italian filmmakers, this was not a problem, because they always dubbed their dialogue in postproduction. But we were recording direct sound, which required complete silence. However, by a bit of technical wizardry that was overcome.

The next problem was the hum. The studio lamps are normally run from a DC generator, but Cinecitta had alternating, not direct, current, causing a hum that the sound recordist was picking up. Fortunately there was an unused DC generator that was put back into service. After a few other adjustments, including changing all the bulbs in the lamps, the sound department pronounced themselves happy. The Italians thought we were being difficult.

I had vaguely noticed that the crew on the shooting floor seemed to be getting larger. This had not escaped Joe Mankiewicz either, and he called the camera crew to one side, pointed to a gentleman walking by with a broom, and said, "Look, we have been on this movie for three months. Can any of you tell me what that guy over there does on the unit? Have you seen him before?"

We admitted that we hadn't, and we didn't know what he did. "Right," said Joe.

"Neither do I." He promptly sent for the production manager and had the entire unit, with the exception of the British and the Americans, assembled in the stage at lunchtime.

A crowd of approximately one hundred were gathered there. Joe went to every man and asked the ones he did not recognize what their job was. Subsequently a good forty of them were immediately dismissed. It appeared that the Italians had been sneaking family and friends onto the payroll with the connivance of the Italian unit manager, who was presumably pocketing a percentage. The Italians, in their usual philosophic way, smiled and waved their hands about. "Oh well, it was worth a try," was their attitude. A strict check was kept after that.

After about a month we went up to the port of Livorno to shoot a small sequence with the principals. From time to time we had been instructing Joe in that very English of things, Cockney rhyming slang, which amused him greatly but which compounded even further the American production manager's belief that he had sold his soul to the British devils. Joe also confessed that the game of cricket had always interested him but he didn't understand it. I think most of us have from time to time tried to explain the rules to other nationalities and have come to realize that it was a hopeless task. It even sounds crazy to me when I try to explain it.

The best we could do was to promise to take him to a match at Lords cricket ground on our return. Which we did and had a most enjoyable day, although I doubt that he was any the wiser about it afterwards.

We returned to the studio and got on with the movie, which was nearly finished. Columbia, which was backing it, wanted it completed quickly, as they already had a premiere date set. So we finished it, and all that remained was a really splendid end-of-picture party thrown by

Joe at which he gave a speech, some of which was in rhyming slang, much to our delight. Even Johnny Johnson smiled (albeit a trifle stiffly, I thought).

It was virtually the last black-and-white picture I was involved in, but one I will always remember for many reasons, not the least of which was the privilege of working with Joseph L. Mankiewicz.

# CHAPTER 10

~

# Roots

*The Roots of Heaven* was a film that had many rich ingredients going for it. First, there were two legendary names as producer and director, Darryl F. Zanuck and John Huston. Then there was an international cast consisting of Trevor Howard, Errol Flynn (in his last film), Orson Welles, Eddie Albert, Juliette Greco, and a selection of experienced European actors. The technicians were also international, a mixture of English, American, French, and Italian.

The script was based on a Pulitzer Prize–winning novel by the French author Romain Gary and dealt primarily with the survival of the African elephant. After the first couple of weeks the mixture of technicians was working well. International filmmakers have a common bond irrespective of nationality and language, and a communication of their own. The "we are all in this together" attitude also helped.

We were shooting in CinemaScope once again, but this time using a new lens system. Bausch and Lomb had successfully combined the photographing and the "squeezing" lenses into one, thereby dispensing with the additional focus puller used when they were separate entities. Unfortunately, in so doing, they had had to sacrifice definition. Compared to a normal lens, the combination was not really "sharp." But as the standard remained constant and there was no direct comparison, it sufficed. Later on Bausch and Lomb did improve the overall quality quite considerably.

The lenses themselves were cumbersome, and as they varied in size they each required a different front fitting to the camera sound "blimp." That meant further ancillary equipment. The blimp itself, which was normally black, I had painted white to help reflect the strong sunlight and reduce the inside temperature. But we still had to employ the old "refrigerator" technique of a wet towel draped over the magazine to keep the film sufficiently cool. All in all, we had approximately fifty-two boxes to be transported every day to the various locations. In that extremely hot, dry, and dusty African climate it could become quite arduous.

Another element added to the use of CinemaScope was the markings on the camera ground glass. On looking through you normally saw an area heavily etched upon it, denoting the framing required for whichever format you were using. The aspect ratio for CinemaScope was 2.33 to 1, but at that time not all theaters were equipped with the necessary projection equipment. Consequently, reduction prints were also made to convert it to the current wide screen ratio of 1.85 to 1 that most theaters could cope with. This meant further markings on the ground glass. In fact, the impossible was being asked, to wit, to compose correctly for two different ratios. As the Mitchell cameras of that time still employed the viewfinder system when actually shooting the scene, they also had to be marked accordingly. A vague instruction was "to keep any important action in the center of the picture" so it would not be lost regardless of the ratio it was shown in. As can be imagined this made certain situations extremely difficult.

Later on it was decreed that the soundtrack areas would also be so marked, adding further problems. As a colleague remarked, "Looking through the camera reminds me of the layout of a railroad terminus." To add further to the camera operator's problems, when using a wide-angle lens such as the 35-mm and 40-mm, it was necessary to use an additional reduction lens on the viewfinder to accommodate the extra width required. The poor optical quality of this lens did not improve the viewfinder, whose quality was indifferent in the first place. But we managed.

The tactics of our Italian production manager, who had elected to mount a large public address system on top of the production office through which he announced his orders and general instructions, did not help matters. The unit did not appreciate this kind of military behavior in a bamboo-walled camp, but his attitude did promote bonding in the crew. It was not long before some wit had christened the camp "Zanuckville." The production designer—ever the rebel—had driven his Land Rover through one of the walls as a protest. Not too much could be said to him about that because of his seniority and the fact that he alleged that it was an accident.

It was about that time that the French contingent started to become a little restless. We had been away from civilization for about a month, and it appeared that their carnal desires were getting the better of them. There had been, it seemed, a few skirmishes with the local beauties, which usually commenced by putting them under a shower (a suspended bucket full of holes) and dousing them with a dilute solution of Lysol. Whether the ladies had refused any further cooperation was not known, but it culminated in the French requesting the production manager to ship in a selection of ladies of dubious virtue from Paris. I think he got out of that one by pointing out that no such contingency had been allowed for in the budget.

With such a polyglot collection of nationalities the matter of the cuisine was bound to arise. We were informed that this had been taken into consideration and that a chef skilled in the cooking of the various countries had been engaged. It was a pretty thankless task. In general he coped with it well, but met his Waterloo when he announced that, as a special gesture to the English, he had prepared one of their delicacies, a bread and butter pudding. When served it had the consistency of concrete. All attempts with various sharp instruments made no impression at all.

In frustration one of the camera crew took a large piece and hurled it at the chef, who happened to be a few tables away. This unfortunately coincided with our bald-headed Italian accountant at the next table rising to his feet and getting it right between the eyes. It laid him out, necessitating medical attention from the unit doctor. Inexplicably, it was never served again.

The unfortunate accountant had already come in for some practical joking. It was seldom that we needed any money, as there was very little to spend it on except for the odd bottle or some cigarettes, but upon being requested for a small sum it was invariably "locked in the safe" and he didn't have the key at that moment. In fact, everything was locked in the inaccessible safe. It was removed one night and secreted in the ladies' toilet. This prompted a general hue and cry and even the local police were brought in. The accountant by this time had gone into a decline and had taken to his bed. Its eventual discovery some two days later led to some nasty suspicious looks from the production manager every time he saw the camera crew.

Orson Welles had a relatively small part in the picture. I think it was in the period of his life when he was mainly working to raise money for his own productions; I believe that he was partly through *Othello* and had need of funds to continue. This colored his attitude toward any picture that was not his own, as he obviously regarded it as simply a means to an end and tended to be rather impatient to get on with it. That led to a few minor clashes with Huston, whose laid-back style did not include much haste. The upshot was that Welles was inclined to be rather brusque and intolerant of other people's problems, and not particularly popular.

One shot required him to be leaning over a table and accidentally shot in the behind by an elephant gun supposedly wielded by Trevor Howard. This required his breeches to be specially rigged by the special effects department. Minute explosive charges were set to blow outwards, just making harmless holes in said breeches. Whether by accident or design (it was never proved), two of them blew inwards, making small perforations in Mr. Welles's bottom. As can be imagined, this caused a certain furor, as he had to be assisted to first aid and took no further part in the day's proceedings. There did not appear to be a lot of sympathy from the crew, the general opinion being that he had it coming to him. After that, he appeared to be somewhat chastened. A rumor circulated that Huston, himself a great practical joker, was the instigator, but needless to say, it was also not proven.

Darryl Zanuck, when he was with us, would stay around the shooting most of the day, and it was a regular sight to see this very small man, once known as "The Czar of all the Rushes," constantly by Huston's side in conference. It was a rather bizarre spectacle as Huston at six feet, six inches, with cigar rampant, towered above him. Whatever they used to discuss made no effect upon Huston, who did precisely what he wanted to do. Zanuck had a habit of dropping his twelve-inch-long cigar from his mouth; after stooping to pick it up and then attempting to resume the conversation he would find that Huston had moved away. In the end, doubtless frustrated by this, he gave up, and we did not see much more of him until we reached Paris for the studio interiors.

A newly appointed publicity man, one Al Hicks, arrived at the local airstrip, where he was met by Zanuck. Unfortunately, Al, suffering from the condition charitably known as "a touch of the Old Trouble" brought about by the refreshment offered on the long journey, stumbled down the aircraft steps and measured his length at Zanuck's feet. Somehow he managed to survive this inauspicious start and remained with us.

Errol Flynn had arrived with a sixteen-year-old named Beverly Adland, who, he said, came from a circus family specializing in acrobatics. This understandably received a certain amount of ribald comment, which in no way abashed Mr. Flynn. He seemed to be used to that sort of thing. When not working, he and Beverly would cycle through the native villages where they would often pose for anybody that had a camera. He would appear on the set in the early morning bearing a glass with a tissue over it to keep out the flying insects. This turned out to be a gin and tonic and obviously constituted his breakfast. He was at all times very genial and was forever showing me expensive watches and lighters, and so forth, given to him by his various lady conquests through the years. Sadly, he died shortly after the picture was finished.

There were quite a few "characters" on that film. Not the least was Patrick Leigh Fermor, an Irish writer who had written quite a lot of the screenplay. He was there in a standby capacity, in case there were any revisions to be made. As there seldom were, he spent a great deal of his time beneath the shade of a nearby plane tree, complete with book and bottle. It was generally understood that script revisions would be done before midday, because his customary long siesta rendered him unavailable for any creative output in the afternoon. He was very charming and amusing, and on one occasion, when being gently reprimanded for drinking a whole bottle of wine, he observed that "One swallow does not make a summer, dear boy." He came and went at regular intervals throughout the production, appearing, it would seem, when it suited him.

The other noteworthy character was a tall, rangy, and verbose Californian named Fred Etcheverry. Fred, it was rumored, had been a sort of nursemaid and bodyguard to Zanuck's children when they were young. He was on the film as a special effects expert and did not do anything by halves. When Fred gave us an explosion it felt as if the whole of Africa shook. He was a firm believer in the efficacy of Scotch whisky, claiming that it would prevent all tropical ills. He was, in fact, the only man I ever met who would water his very large whisky by standing under the shower. In the evening he would regale us with tales of Old Hollywood and was generally entertaining.

We needed this kind of thing in our leisure moments; the days were very exacting. The daytime temperature was around 90°F and dry and dusty. Any time a vehicle drove by we would disappear in a cloud of dust. This also did not do our equipment a lot of good; it required a lot of maintenance. African dust seems to penetrate everywhere. To help to combat the heat a little we used to start the shooting day around 7:00 A.M. and continue nonstop to around 2:00 P.M., when the heat was at its worst. For a couple of hours we would seek what shelter we could out of the sun and recommence for another two hours or so around four o'clock. It was very dangerous to be in that sun without a hat and a neck covering. The face was usually generously covered with pan makeup base procured from the makeup dept, making us appear like Red Indians.

One of the actors, Eddie Albert, did venture onto a hilltop when not working without the necessary covering and sustained severe sunstroke, which put him in to the sick bay for a couple of days.

However, even in those conditions our morale was pretty good. As I have stated before, the English all knew each other, the rest of the unit worked well together, and there was a generally good atmosphere. I think the overall conditions helped a little, as we were all in the same boat, as it were.

Toward the end of the location I suffered a touch of dysentery, which I was a trifle prone to, and had to spend three or four days crawling between my bed and the somewhat basic toilet. It was no help that the temperature in my hut was around 100°F, so I lay there in a pool of sweat, not feeling too great. Having had it before, I knew that the cure was a form of chalk tablet called Sulphaguenadine. The unit French doctor thought otherwise and insisted that what I needed was mint tea at regular intervals administered by his nurse (known incidentally, as "The Doctor's Dilemma"). The doctor himself had not shown himself to be overly proficient and there had been dark mutterings that he had been struck off the French Medical Registrar for dubious practices. Be that as it may, he wasn't doing me much good. I told the director of photography, Oswald Morris, what I actually needed, and he broke into the medical stores himself and got the correct pill. I think that the doctor thought that the mint tea and the nurse had done the trick, never discovering that Ossie had fixed it.

We eventually shot our final scene in Equatorial Africa, not without a certain amount of relief, and began packing to return to Paris. John Huston and a few cronies decided to stay on and do some elephant hunting. At least that was what he said.

So we enplaned for Paris. It was April by now, and I can still recall landing at Orly Airport and tasting the cool, non-dust-ridden air. Whatever else it may have contained, it was like a tonic after the three months of African airless heat and dust. After finding suitable accommodation we established ourselves at the Boulogne studios and awaited the arrival of the director. He elected not to arrive until some four days later, and after checking and maintaining our equipment, we spent that time seeing Paris and generally adjusting ourselves back to Europe. Anyway, we felt we had earned it.

Huston arrived and we started shooting in the studio. In accordance with their lifestyle, the French work from 12:00 noon until 8:00 P.M. when in the studios. Very civilized, we thought, as it enabled us to eat late in the evening and enjoy a little of the City of Light without having to get up early in the morning. The shooting day was nonstop, with a constant running buffet laid on in the stages. I never did quite get used to going to two large urns expecting to get tea or coffee and finding red or white wine, which the French *machinoux* got through with great rapidity. At the time M. Mendes-France was the French prime minister, and in all the Metro stations were large posters exhorting the French to drink milk under the banner "Sobrieté est Santé." I never did think that he stood much of a chance.

John Huston, as I have mentioned, was a great practical joker and could be a trifle sadistic. He decided to call both Errol Flynn and Trevor

Howard at twelve sharp one day but we never (as he well knew) got around to using them until around seven o'clock in the evening. As both Messrs. Flynn and Howard had a well-known predilection for alcohol and had become bored stiff with just hanging around, they were in a sorry state by the time we came to shoot on them. The set was an extremely small native hut where Trevor, who was playing the local district commissioner, sat working at his desk. Enter Flynn, who has to tell Trevor that "A man and a woman are waiting for you in the village." On receipt of this intelligence, Trevor rises and leaves. We never actually got that far. There was only a very narrow entrance to the hut and quite a number of small lamps and a series of ancillary equipment narrowed the actual working space even more. The sequence went as follows:

Take 1. Flynn endeavors without success to enter. He cannons off the side of the entrance twice and gives up.

Take 2. This time he gets through by running but his momentum takes some of the lights etc. with him.

Take 3. This time he makes it more or less and gets to his mark, swaying slightly, and can't remember his line.

Take 4. Repeat of above, except he says "Oh, fuck it!"

Take 5. Aborted. Trevor has the giggles.

Take 6. Flynn gets in cleanly, gets to his mark and says: "There's a man up a woman waiting for you in the village."

By now, of course, everyone was in hysterics, including, to his credit, Flynn himself. Huston appeared to be having a seizure. We abandoned it after that and reshot it correctly the following day. Huston printed all the failed takes, and when we viewed them next day with rushes they were even funnier.

It was decided that it would be in everyone's best interests that, when he was not working and in order to keep him sober, Trevor should have a Minder. The person selected for this thankless task was Zanuck's secretary, Maggie Shipway. She quite rightly refused to go around with Trevor, but he had to tell her where he was going and leave a telephone number for contact if required. The other proviso was that Errol Flynn should not accompany him. This seemed to work surprisingly well until Maggie had a late-night phone call from the proprietor of a night club in St. Germain in voluble French asking for assistance, as "Mr.

*Jerry Lewis and me,* One More Time, *M-G-M, Borehamwood Studios.*

*David Niven and Joanna Pettet,* Casino Royale. *I'm looking through the camera.*

*The demolished square in Saigon for* The Quiet American.

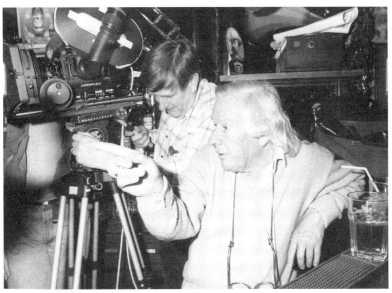

*Shooting a Fuji demo reel for their new fast stock.*

*Shooting a prestige corporate for Rolls Royce at St. Andrews' famous golf course.*

*A drink commercial in North Africa. I'm at the camera.*

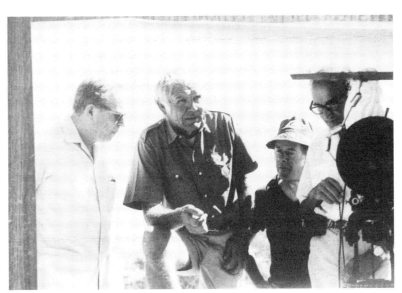

Living Free *in Kenya: (l to r) Carl Foreman, Jack Couffeur, me, and Wolfgang Suchitsky.*

*Night sequence in the Malta tank, a model submarine on fire for* A Twist of Sand.

*Aboard a Greek navy destroyer for* The Guns of Navarone: *(l to r) Sandy Mackendrick, Ossie Morris, and me.*

*With Bob Huke, the director of photography, on* The War Lover. *Shirley Anne Field is in the background.*

*Waiting for the camera equipment to arrive in Seoul, Korea.*

'Oward" was proving difficult. On arrival she found Trevor sitting on the floor wearing a large bass drum around his neck like a ruff. It appeared he had volunteered to conduct the band, slipped, and gone through it head first. Maggie, having paid for the damage, took him back to his hotel with no further trouble.

Shooting in Paris had been delightful and we felt it more than made up for the tough African location. We finally finished on schedule and had an end-of-picture party on board the pleasure boat *Bateau Rouge* on the Seine. Zanuck actually gave me one of his twelve-inch non-nicotine cigars, but the sheer weight of it was enough for me.

Making films under these conditions can be stressful. The fact that seventy-odd people—in this case, of mixed nationalities—have to live in a camp miles from civilization as we know it, and in extreme heat and otherwise oppressive climate, can tax the morale severely. Working those long hours would be tiring even in more temperate surroundings. The sporadic arrival of mail from home resembled mail call in the Armed Forces during the war.

Much responsibility is thrown upon the various heads of departments to keep things on an even keel within their own group, and to create the equable atmosphere that is essential to keep the production proceeding smoothly. It is far from easy. On *Roots of Heaven* it worked well.

# CHAPTER 11

~

# Directors I Have Known

It is possible to categorize directors only up to a certain point. Some are tyrannical and difficult to work with, some are amiable and easy. Some are talented, some are not. Some would lean heavily on their senior technicians to cover up their own inadequacies; others would endeavor to bluff their way through. They all have their own individual approaches, and it is pleasant to work with one who knows what he wants and how to go about it.

John Huston certainly was that. He was an ostensibly relaxed director with an extremely shrewd mind when it came to casting, his philosophy being that if you assemble the right ingredients and mix them all together, the rest would take care of itself. This also applied to his senior technicians (i.e., the director of photography, production designer, sound recordist, first assistant director, etc.). His attitude toward the actors was that they had been especially selected for their parts, were very highly paid, and that they knew just as much as he did of how to go about it. He regarded himself as merely the catalyst. On *Roots of Heaven* he proved his point.

Don Chaffey was rather different. Don had a deserved reputation for bringing in movies on schedule and budget with the minimum of fuss. His abilities had been noted by Disney, for whom he made several successful pictures, *Greyfriars Bobby* and *The Three Lives of Thomasina* among them. The word "art" was not mentioned in his presence. Tall, rangy, and with a shambling gait, he was hirsute and overall possessed a slightly villainous aspect. His home address was in Cutthroat Lane, Folkestone, and he was part owner of a trawler on which he spent a certain amount of his spare time. Don was one of the boys, an extrovert and a great raconteur. He was never happier than with an audience, regaling them with his stories and reminiscences.

A *Twist of Sand* was a tale of derring-do, taken from a novel, and most of the action took place in Southwest Africa and the seas and coasts thereof. Logistically and economically it was impractical to go there, so the Mediterranean was chosen, the base to be in Malta. Malta also had a large tank suitable for shooting models, of which we had plenty, and was built on top of a cliff with a natural horizon. We started with the models, the filming of which was a leisurely affair—shooting on average two shots a day. It took the special effects department some time to get the shots organized.

This necessitated long intervals and protracted lunches during which Don held the floor in full spate. This was known as "Listening with Don at Lunchtime," or we would eat outside and "Listen to Don al fresco." He had a great ability to top anyone else's stories. Whatever tale was told, Don could better it, and his range of knowledge was phenomenal. We put our heads together to see if we could outwit him.

Someone came up with what we were sure was a winner. It was planned that during one of the infrequent pauses I would be asked "how my bees were getting on." That subject would fix him, we thought. The opportunity arose and the question was put. Before I could reply, Don said "Bees? Did you say bees? Well, well. I'm the Chairman of the Folkestone Apiarist Society!" We conceded defeat as graciously as we could and never tried again. He had successfully beaten off all competition and from then on continued to have the floor to himself. But he was nothing if not entertaining

In between these little diversions we did some work. The model tank was reasonably large and not too deep. Its main drawback was that it was salt water pumped up from the adjacent sea. That in itself was not a problem, but the tank was situated right above the main island sewer outlet. If the wind was blowing on shore the same time as the water was being pumped in, a "shit slick" would appear in the tank. This invariably led to some spirited dialogue between our production office and the tank's owners, causing a hold-up while it was dispersed. This sometimes led to another prolonged lunch and another dose of Don in full flow.

At one point he devised a shot that involved the camera on the prow of a one-fifth scale model of a high-speed launch and shooting a subjective shot of the craft weaving its way through dangerous waters past rocks and shoals. There was just room for Don and myself on board. We cruised round the tank, wallowing in the rough seas created by the wave machines. At a given point a tip tank was to disgorge its load of many tons of water to create an even heavier sea. Unfortunately the cue was given too late, and instead of sweeping into the sea ahead of us, it hit us fair and square from behind. We promptly sank to the bottom of the five-foot-deep tank.

The still photographer took a picture of the boat with just its radio mast above water and Don and me, still sitting, with just our heads protruding. We scrambled ashore, and the next ten minutes was devoted to Don telling the special effects department exactly what he thought of them and their technical prowess. After which we retired for lunch once more while they sorted out the chaos.

That day's Chaffey Lecture was mainly devoted to the general incompetence of the special effects department (rather unfairly) and further reminiscences of their shortcomings on some of his other productions.

He was a great socialite and received numerous invitations to dine out. He was usually on the set first thing in the morning, but one day there was no sign of him. His office was empty, his hotel had not seen him since the previous night. Phone calls were made to some of his known haunts, with no success. As it happened, the first shot that day had been planned the previous evening and special effects had much to do to set it up. So we carried on. He eventually arrived some two hours later, saying that he knew we would not be ready for him yet. His actual whereabouts remained a mystery and it was never disclosed. We decided that it would be better not to ask.

There was seldom, if ever, a dull moment with Don, and, despite the setbacks, we finished on time and he had sustained his justifiable reputation.

And then there was Anthony Mann. A vastly experienced director, he brought his expertise to Norway for *The Heroes of Telemark*. I was allocated to the second unit for this one. It was January, and the conditions were arctic. The players were Kirk Douglas, Richard Harris, Michael Redgrave, and Ulla Jacobsen. The script was based on a true war story of the Nazi heavy water factory in Rjukon and its ultimate destruction.

It needed all of Tony Mann's expertise to deal initially with the cast. Kirk Douglas was obviously a man used to having his own way and not a little arrogant. He frequently refused to do a second take if he thought that his part was all right. In these difficult and bitter conditions, such lack of consideration for the others caused a certain amount of friction. To make matters worse, Douglas and Richard Harris took an instant dislike to one another.

Tony Mann had obviously met similar situations before and he handled it well, but the obvious antipathy between the two main actors sometimes showed on the screen.

My first encounter with the director had been shortly after my arrival. We were covering the landing of several gliders carrying the special commando force that was to attack the factory. Two of them crash on landing and catch fire. The scene required a lot of organization, involving the special effects department and the props rigging a rubber-tire fire in the distance to simulate the crash. I had been told that Tony Mann was somewhat irascible and impatient by nature, and my first meeting seemed to bear this out. He rushed about continually berating the rigging crew, muttering that "they don't seem to understand a goddam word I say." He was a little difficult to follow, as he had a very clipped accent and spoke extremely quickly. He came back to my camera, still muttering about the lack of communication, and half-jokingly I said that it was probably because we had a language barrier. For some reason he found this uproariously funny, and it broke the ice between us. He actually went around telling people what I had said. It seemed to help the situation somewhat, and he calmed down a bit.

Despite his tactful handling, the mutual dislike between Douglas and Harris had not been resolved. On a very open and windy location, Harris accused Douglas of deliberately keeping him waiting. This could possibly have been true; some actors often played the silly game of being the last to arrive on the set, in a misguided gesture of superior status. Given the animosity between these two, it was more than likely. Douglas hotly denied the charge, with the result that they both walked off the location. Tony Mann interpreted this as the producer's problem and sent for him. Enter Benny Fisch, endeavoring to act as mediator while the unit stood around waiting for the next episode. Re-enter Benny to announce that Douglas had gone off in a huff back to his hotel. Tony Mann decided we had other work to do, so we got on with it.

Next day we learned that Douglas had been on the phone to his agent and various other members of the Hollywood hierarchy, trying to have Harris removed and replaced on the film. This was not practical, as we had been shooting for four weeks, and was also not contractually possible. The following day they both reappeared and spent the day like two sulky children. Tony Mann had to work very hard to keep the movie on an even keel. His vast experience of Westerns may have helped, but he managed to ignore—as best he could—their problems and quietly he forced the pace along to enable us to get back on schedule. He was an excellent example of a very professional director at work under very trying climatic conditions. Sometimes the temperature was well below zero, giving us problems keeping the cameras running.

He was, however, responsible for a little light comic relief. He had a pair of fur boots that were kept warm by means of a small electric current generated from a battery in the pocket of his coat. This malfunctioned on several occasions, causing him to retire to warm his feet and getting rather bad tempered in the process. One day the current went straight to his feet instead of his boots, causing him to leap up and down in a sort of bizarre dance. The next day he arrived in alternative attire that at least made him a little calmer. The last we heard of that was, in true directorial style, that he was about to sue the manufacturers.

But, for all his moods, I enjoyed working with him. At least you knew you were with someone who knew all about making movies.

At the other end of the scale was a European director of dubious origin with whom I worked in Israel on *Rebels against the Light,* a story about Arab infiltration in the early days of the country's existence. My first meeting with him was none too auspicious. We first met in a London hotel when he appeared looking as if he had slept in his clothes, his face covered with pieces of toilet paper where he had cut himself shaving. His English was limited and even more so when he became excited, as he did frequently. It soon became obvious that, despite his constant reiteration of his cinema credits, his film knowledge was even more limited than his grasp of the English language. He also name-dropped continually about all his notable friends in Hollywood. This filled me with some foreboding, which was subsequently justified.

He had, however, a good script and an excellent cast, including Tom Bell and Diane Baker. The next six weeks were plain hard work. He had little or no idea how to design and shoot a sequence. Apart from anything else, his floundering was incredibly time-consuming; everything had to be all done for him. Realizing that we were all well aware of his shortcomings, every time things went awry (which was frequently), he endeavored to blame somebody else. As can be imagined, this was not conducive to a good atmosphere or good filmmaking. However, after a week or so of this he had the sense to leave the technicalities and the design of the scenes to us and concentrated on the actors. This was not too popular with them, since they did not hold him in high esteem, but we felt that it was their turn anyway and we just got on with it.

At the end of the picture party he did admit that he could not have made the picture without us. This caused a certain amount of merriment, and I heard Tom Bell mutter "Amen to that!"

This raised yet again the hoary old film-business question, "How on earth did he get the job?" That, I fear, opens up a whole different world to which we humble technicians are not privy. But we can sometimes make an educated guess. And, unfortunately, there have been many such.

The name of Michael Winner is possibly as well known outside the film business as it is within. I worked with Michael on one of his earlier films (which I understand he now affects not to remember) entitled *The Cool Mikado*.

Michael was at his best on this, that is, he was generally unpleasant all round. He fired people at random and could be incredibly rude. The only way to deal with him was to give back as good as he gave. I managed to survive by employing this technique.

As the title suggests, it was a modern musical version of Gilbert and Sullivan. When shooting musical numbers we would always cover it with two cameras. For reasons known only to himself, Michael took a dislike to the second camera operators, no matter how efficient they were, and would not have the same one twice.

On the final day we had one last musical number to shoot, so I called a friend and colleague, one Neil (Ginger) Gemmell. I warned him to be wary of Michael.

At lunchtime we were just leaving the stage, when, sure enough, Michael called him over. I went with him. The dialogue ran as follows:

> Michael ( very pompously): "Now Ginger, I always ask the second camera operator whether he has done anything wrong this morning. Have you?"

Pause while Ginger rubs his chin and looks thoughtful.

> Michael: "Come on now, have you?"
>
> Ginger (very slowly): "Yes, yes, I have."
>
> Michael (triumphantly): "And what was it?"
>
> Ginger: "It was coming down here and working with you in the first place!"

Winner roared with laughter and Ginger could do no wrong from then on in.

But a delightful man named Henry Cornelius, who had directed the highly successful *Genevieve* and possessed an apt sense of humor, made my favorite directorial comment. After the first week's shooting on his debut film, he said to the director of photography, "Do you know, this is the first day that I have really felt that I was not in anyone's way!'

# CHAPTER 12

~

# The Entertainer

I am sure most film technicians have their favorite movies, the ones they enjoyed working on most. Out of the many films I have been involved with, I always recall *The Entertainer* with great affection. It was one in which the chemistry worked with the crew, the actors, and the location.

Based on John Osborne's successful stage play, it starred Laurence Olivier, Shirley Anne Field, Roger Livesey, and Joan Plowright and was directed by Tony Richardson. Tony had just successfully made *Look Back in Anger*, also by Osborne.

The story was about a seedy, third-rate vaudeville comedian, one Archie Rice, played by Olivier, and his lifestyle. It was a somber tale, in fact a tragedy, but a fascinating one. It had a first-rate cast, which—apart from the principals—included Albert Finney, Alan Bates, Brenda de Banzie, and Thora Hird, plus a sharply observed script. The location was in Morecambe, Lancashire, northwest of England, and apart from the odd exterior, mostly shot in the interior of an old theater, the Alhambra. It was but a shadow of its former self, a relic of the Edwardian-era music halls, and just decrepit enough for our purposes. It was to be shot in monochrome by Oswald Morris, B.S.C.

A local beauty contest was required, so we went to Morecambe before the main shooting to photograph it. As beauty contests go, it was nothing untoward but did prompt possibly the worse joke I have ever made. To symbolize the proceedings and give it a bit of much-needed style, a plaster statue of the Venus de Milo was placed by the pool. Unfortunately the plinth was missing. Someone pointed this out and I had to remark that "Thum day her plinth will come." Quite rightly, I was not spoken to for some time.

The crew contained many old friends and quite a few characters. Peter Handford was the sound mixer, an old friend with an impish sense of humor. We had previously worked together on *The Story of Esther Costello*, starring the "Queen of the Cinema," Joan Crawford. A set of a village hall had required Miss Crawford to address a large gathering with the highly original opening line, "I am unaccustomed to speaking in public."

She got no further as a voice from behind the backing where Peter had placed his equipment was heard to say, "And we won't hear you now if you don't speak up!" Miss Crawford was not used to this kind of approach and was a trifle nonplussed. However, she tried again, this time to Peter's satisfaction. Sounds of stifled merriment were heard from behind the backing, and we carried on, albeit a little uncertainly by Miss Crawford.

To give *The Entertainer* the true vaudeville authenticity, a varied additional cast had been assembled. Apparently it was customary in that class of show to include a classical tableau to add a little "tone." This one was to be *Aphrodite Arising from the Foam*. We had a cast of three ladies depicting Brittania, Boadicea, and Aphrodite. They were a very unlikely trio. The lady who played Britannia was of ample proportions, but her mental prowess was in direct inverse ratio to her avoirdupois. She was compliant and monosyllabic. In sharp contrast, Boadicea was thin, neurotic, and garrulous. The upper-crust accent that she affected launched a catch phrase repeated throughout the entire film business. The third member of the troupe was a woman of the world. She had been everywhere, done everything, and belonged to the school of thought holding that men had only one thing on their mind. During the whole of the Morecambe location I don't think that philosophy was ever put to the test. Unwittingly, they were all very funny.

Shirley Anne Field and I had become good friends and, one evening, after viewing dailies in a local cinema, went out to dinner. We returned to the hotel to find several members of the unit plus *les dames du tableau* having a nightcap at the bar. We joined them, and Shirley regaled them with the story of her early life in an orphanage, as she was wont to do. During this discourse I got up to buy a round of drinks and went round the group taking the order. When I came to the garrulous Boadicea (who had been unable to get a word in for once), she deliberated and announced in her best accent "May I have a Bowjolly?" I paused, thinking this through. To assist me she added, "It's wayne, you know." I went to the bar rather hurriedly. Since then that quotation has been used extensively throughout the film business by many people when ordering a bottle of Beaujolais wine, unaware of its origin.

The large Brittania had been the butt of many good-natured jokes. Once, when she asked where the dailies were going to be one evening, somebody told her to just get into the open MG parked outside, for a lift to the cinema. The MG was mine. She was firmly ensconced when I got there, and as I drove along the car listed to one side, the suspension complaining loudly. She weighed, roughly, 240 pounds. On arrival she attempted to get out but to no avail, as she was well and truly stuck. I had to call for assistance, and it took three of us to eventually pry her out, myself cursing every time something got disturbed on my precious motor car. Meanwhile, as we had parked in the main road, we had collected a crowd of spectators who cheered every inch of the extraction. We were late getting to the dailies and not too popular. After that I was told that Brittania referred to me as "that nice boy who gave me a lift." She must have wondered why I never repeated the offer.

Peter Handford's sense of humor was not to lie dormant for too long. At the beginning of every shot the number board, on which was written all the relevant information—the scene and take numbers, the photographic effect, etc.—was presented in front of the camera and clapped in order for the editors to synchronize the sound in the cutting rooms. In large letters across the top was emblazoned the film's title, *The Entertainer*. Through habit, it was seldom noticed as to what was precisely written on it. It was the clapper boy's job to attend to all that. Peter, aware of this, had a special number board made up exactly the same except that the title had been changed to *The Undertaker*. With the collaboration of the camera department this was duly presented before each shot as normal. The point was made—it was a good two weeks before Tony Richardson inquired, "How long has that been on there?" Even the editors had not noticed it. Everyone feigned innocence, of course. But Handford, biding his time, struck again.

Roger Livesey, through years of declaiming from the theatrical stage, had developed a strong fruity voice and had a habit of clearing his throat loudly before each take with a loud cough. A new number board appeared. This time it bore the inscription *The Cough Syrup Story*. That also lasted for about four days until Olivier spotted it and roared with laughter. Once again it was an apparent mystery to all.

It has been my experience that, when working with a really professional crew who knew their jobs thoroughly (and other peoples as well), things go relatively smoothly. There usually seemed time for a few jokes that helped jolly things along without in any way interfering with the production and it helped to create a good atmosphere. I really think it did help in this case, particularly with Tony Richardson, despite the fact that he was a trifled puzzled by it, being more used to the slightly heavier ambience of the theatre. He had directed only one picture before and was a little in awe of Olivier. But everyone pitched in to help with any problems.

In the palmy days of 1959 we worked civilized hours and there was time to enjoy a relaxing evening after a day's work. Odd evenings we took a stroll round the local public houses, which were still full of holidaymakers enjoying themselves. We managed to get some of them to sing and tell stories, all of which Peter Handford was covertly recording on a small tape machine in his pocket, the microphone concealed behind the lapel of his jacket.

We finished up in grand style one evening in a small back-street inn with a crowd whom the management seemed unable to get to leave after the appointed hour. They eventually effectively dealt with the crowd by the simple expediency of slinging a bucket of undiluted carbolic on the floor. It worked splendidly.

Peter transferred that evening's performances to disk, and it has provided many an entertaining evening since.

I saw the picture again on television recently. Quite a lot of the scenes I could hardly remember—after all, it was made nearly forty years ago. But it did evoke some very happy memories.

# CHAPTER 13

# Commercials and Corporates

My introduction to commercials came by chance. A clapper boy, an enterprising lad who had worked with me on three films in South Africa, rang me one evening some weeks after our return. It seemed that he was now involved with a new commercial production company in Chelsea; would I like to come to their office to meet the director and discuss a job? I agreed—a trifle reluctantly, because, although I knew this lad to be bright and ambitious, he was also something of a practical joker. However, having nothing better to do that day, I went along. As it turned out, it was genuine.

I was introduced to the director and two gentlemen from the J. Walter Thompson advertising agency. The product was Strongbow cider, and a beach was required to shoot on. After an hour or so that for me consisted mainly of listening and occasionally answering a technical question, they decided to repair for lunch. This lasted for the better part of three hours, during which time an inordinate amount of alcohol was consumed, but little more discussed about the commercial itself. I was to learn later that this was common practice. We agreed to meet the following day at Thompson's offices in Berkeley Square.

This turned out to be a much larger assembly, consisting of four or five agency members plus their client (Mr. Strongbow) and their creative staff. The script and storyboard were discussed at great length before all was agreed. Then the question of the location of the beach was discussed. It had seemed to me that all that was needed was a fairly long stretch unimpeded by buildings, pylons, and so forth, and I could think of at least half a dozen suitable places in Britain. I said so, but it was obviously the wrong thing to say. They were determined to go to foreign climes, come what may.

For the next half-hour we traveled the world, everywhere from Cape Town to Florida, bypassing only the Seychelles and Malaysia. Eventually it was agreed that we would shoot in Agadir, Morocco, which apparently had some beautiful beaches. At the time I was a trifle puzzled about the choice of this particular venue, and it wasn't until some time later that I learned that the wife of the creative head of the agency had always wanted to go there for a holiday. This was a golden opportunity, all expenses paid. So that was that, and we repaired for the obligatory lunch. I was starting to learn about a whole new "Alice in Wonderland" world.

A week later we left from the London airport aboard a chartered aircraft. There seemed to be a few odd people aboard who were certainly not film technicians, and the agency people didn't know them either. I eventually discovered they were friends of my old friend, the clapper boy, and had just come along for the ride. There were spare seats to be had; in fact my girlfriend was occupying one of them. But the presence of the stray personnel was to lead to a little trouble later on.

We arrived at Agadir to find that, overnight, a semihurricane had occurred, rendering the beach a sodden wreck with palm trees and general detritus distributed everywhere. The whole shooting area was a shambles. A team of locals was hastily recruited and a large scale cleaning-up operation took place. Palm trees were relocated and in a few hours it was presentable enough to shoot on. The shoot itself went off without further incident, and three days later we were on the plane back to London. Our additional passengers, who had disappeared immediately we arrived, reappeared in time to join us. On arrival at London they were questioned and thoroughly searched and subsequently detained, as a large amount of cannabis was found in their possession. This was obviously the reason for their Moroccan trip.

There was one more day's shooting in the studio. The final shot was of our hero drinking a pint of cider in one fell swoop. The camera moved in close to his face as he took the final swallow. This was the sixth take. He took the final drink and promptly threw up, all over me and the camera. Not saying a lot for the product, I thought.

However, that particular job led to further work with the same production company and commenced an association with the J. Walter Thompson advertising agency that continued for some years all over the world. As I began to meet more advertising people I realized that they were very much in a world of their own. And as I did more commercials I became aware of the miscellany of people who were involved. A lot of them very talented, including a smattering of definite "head cases," and not a few poseurs.

These latter types would sometimes appear on a shoot clad in curious items of clothing. One particular gentleman would turn up in the height of summer sporting a full-length fur coat and declaim at large on all aspects of commercial filmmaking in a very loud voice. He would return after a long alcoholic lunch, promptly fall asleep, and snore before being assisted out by his colleagues. I was assured by them that he was a genius. It seemed that the more eccentric character you portrayed, the more they thought of you. There were quite a few of them.

In between some of the more outlandish ideas from the agencies, of which there were many, came a few interesting trips. One of the most enjoyable was in Florence. It was at the time that cigarette advertising was still permissible on TV and in the theater, and this one was to feature the painter Pietro Annigoni.

He was a remarkable character who was immediately recognized and acclaimed everywhere he went. Everyone addressed him as "maestro" and practically genuflected when he appeared, invariably attired in a black cloak and beret. This was obviously his public "front," as he was in fact a modest man and easy to talk to. He had painted Queen Elizabeth's picture a few years before, and, because there had been one or two "anti" reactions to it at the time, he worried about it still, even asking us what we thought of its execution.

He was that rare animal, a rich painter, having recently accepted some very lucrative commissions. It was generally agreed that he had no idea how rich he was. A small rather furtive-looking business manager was in charge of all that. We shot in Annigoni's main studio, which was literally strewn with his drawings, sketches, and "doodlings."

The manager never took his eyes off it all, probably thinking that we would pocket something given half a chance, as undoubtedly they were quite valuable. There was no need; Il Maestro presented the director and me with large line drawings of his favorite model, personally signed. Mine graces the wall of my sitting room to this day.

At the end of the shoot he took us to his favorite restaurant up in the Tuscan hills where, of course, he was treated like royalty, and the food and drink were magnificent. I noticed that no bill arrived and no money changed hands. We were told afterwards that the meal was at the restaurant's expense, it being a singular honor to have the Great Man as a guest (and his friends, of course).

Unfortunately this very expensive and visually stunning commercial was never shown, on television. The whole campaign had been conceived around the idea of getting internationally known figures from the arts to be featured in different films, but I was given to understand that the expense became excessive and the whole concept was therefore abandoned. I was disappointed, as I had looked forward to doing the whole series with such luminaries as Salvador Dali and Gerald Durrell, among others, as had been discussed. Still, it was a thoroughly enjoyable experience, and the film was eventually shown in theaters.

At this moment in time I was being offered a lot of commercial work, which was welcome because the feature film situation was not particularly brilliant. Then, out of the blue, came a chance to do a corporate film. The timing of this was rather fortuitous. Commercial companies accustomed to working with particular technicians took it badly when they turned down work. There was a good deal of the personality cult involved. Fortunately the corporate offer coincided with a lull in the work from my commercial contacts, so I was able to do this without upsetting anybody. Anyway, I felt I needed a break from commercials to help regain my sanity even if they were lucrative.

In most cases corporate films were for in-house screenings. They could be training films, or explanations of new techniques, for example. Later on I was to do corporate films for clients ranging from banks to breweries. This one was for Malaysia and the subject was palm oil, which they exported in vast quantities. The director and I set off for Kuala Lumpur, where we met up with the upper echelon of the company and discussed the film in detail. They were charming people and, once having explained what they expected from the film, gave us carte blanche. The first week's shooting was to be in Jahore, right down in the south of Malaysia across from Singapore. We decided to stay there and journey across the causeway daily to Malaya. It was there that we became aware of the different approaches to bureaucracy.

On our first crossing, the Singapore Customs and Immigration people inspected our paperwork and equipment closely. After satisfying themselves, they never stopped us again, just waved us through. At the Malaysian end it was a very different story. Twice as many officials buzzed around our car, taking far longer than the Singaporeans did. They repeated this on our return journey and went through the same procedure every day. No amount of protestation would deter them. We were to discover that Malaysia was riddled with this kind of thing, a hangover it seemed of the British judiciary. But they were all absolutely charming.

While filming in the palm tree forests, we were offered tremendous hospitality. The overseers would invite us to their homes for a meal and to meet their families. They maintained that, since we were strangers to their country, we must be made to feel at home. And we received the utmost cooperation all the time. But anything remotely to do with officialdom got bogged down in paperwork, permits, and so on. I would have liked a particular item of camera equipment that I knew was available, only to find that it belonged to a certain government department and that it would take up to three months to get the necessary permission. I managed without it.

After we had finished in Jahore we drove north via Kuala Lumpur to Ipoh, along dirt roads amid large areas of forest. Sometimes over the treetops a red flag could be seen flying over a village. These signaled the local Communists, but at that time they were giving no trouble. Ipoh turned out to be a colonial gem. We arrived in the dark at the Station Hotel. The car headlights swept round the railway station and illuminated a prewar full-size holiday poster informing us that "Skegness Is So Bracing!" The hotel itself was pure Somerset Maugham, complete with wide verandahs and whirligig fans. Judging by their age, I think the staff were the originals as well. Once more we spent a very pleasant four days shooting in and around the town, the people as helpful and courteous as ever. Then off to Borneo.

This meant going back to Kuala Lumpur and flying due south to Kota Kinabalu, capital of Sabah on the island of Borneo. One overnight stay and then we were flying over the width of the island to the port of Sandakan. Flying over thick forest, we were told that there were still headhunting tribes down there, and in fact a light aircraft had made a foreced landing there a short while ago and nothing had been heard or found of the passengers. We couldn't land at Sandakan too quickly for me.

Sandakan is a port and a little commercial city. The small harbor was crowded; among the boats we saw a couple of oil rigs. At the time the French were carrying out oil exploration, but I understand that they subsequently abandoned it.

We were in need of some money, so I took our travelers checks to the local bank. The English manager greeted me very enthusiastically. He was obviously pleased to see a new face. I explained what we were doing there. It was about 10:00 A.M. He glanced at his watch and, opening a desk drawer, produced a jumbo size bottle of gin. Would I care for a drop? I explained that it was a trifle early for me, so he just helped himself to a large one. This is what comes of living in the far-flung colonies I thought. However, he was most helpful with local information and invited us to lunch at the country club the next day, which was a Sunday.

We had already decided to give ourselves a day off anyway, so we met up with him there. It was a typical ex-pats club, complete with restaurant, bar, and swimming pool. Our host, smartly attired in lightweight blazer and flannels, met us and pressed us to accept an aperitif. It would seem that he himself had started a little earlier. He regaled us with his life story, including the fact that his wife was away in Singapore, which probably explained his somewhat intemperate behavior. The curry lunch was excellent, and the whole thing was finished off in grand style as the bank manager, a trifle wobbly by this time, missed his footing and fell straight into the swimming pool. I noticed that the surrounding guests reacted only slightly to this, giving the impression that it was a fairly regular occurrence. Apparently unfazed, he hauled himself out of the water and went to change his clothes.

He returned clad in a bathrobe, made no reference to the incident, and ordered another drink. I kept a straight face with great difficulty.

However, he did supply most of our social life there, including a splendid boat trip with lunch on board.

After leaving Sandakan (once more viewing the intervening forest with apprehension), we returned to Singapore, finishing off with a wonderful night trip around the island on board one of the palm-oil tankers. Then it was a final night in the famous Raffles Hotel and a dinner with our sponsors before flying back to England the next day. It had been a most successful and enjoyable trip.

There was a lot to be said for this type of filmmaking. The unit usually consisted at most of six or seven people, meaning it could be very mobile and did not have the top brass breathing down its collective neck all the time. It is normal to shoot in 16 mm, so the equipment is less bulky. We made our own decisions as we went along and decided on our working hours. There is no sign of production managers worried about the schedule, or advertising agencies muddying the waters with their demands and pretensions. We were, in fact, our own bosses, and, then as now, generally the subject matter was very interesting.

So, on and off in the next couple of years, I managed to do a few more of them with different companies. Financially it was not as rewarding as commercials or feature films, but the working environment amply made up for that. I was always pleased when asked to do one.

# CHAPTER 14

~

# Children and Animals

I believe it was W. C. Fields who said, "Never work with children and animals." I can readily appreciate that. From an actor's point of view it meant that they can capture all the attention. From a film technician's angle, it means trying to get them to do something.

Certain animals can be unpredictable. Jimmy Chipperfield of the famous circus family had a jaguar that had been born at Jimmy's menagerie and was his special pet. We had it on the set of Disney's *In Search of the Castaways* at Pinewood Studios, where it roamed freely in our artificial jungle and was put back into its large cage at night. One day Jimmy was wearing a new lounge suit because he was due at a private function that evening. Having locked the animal's cage door, he turned toward us, his back to the cage. There was a subdued roar and a loud exclamation from Jimmy as his smart suit peeled away from his body, severed completely and neatly in two. The jaguar had ripped it from the back. Miraculously, Jimmy was not even scratched, but what looked like a comedy scene could have been extremely serious. Jimmy's comment was, "I have always said, never trust them completely, however well you think you know them." And this from someone I know for a fact was the kindest and most understanding of men with all animals.

Jack Couffer, who directed *Living Free* for Columbia, did have the ability to read them. We had a whole range of lions from small cubs to fully grown adults. Jack was very aware that a lot of time could be wasted waiting for them to do what was wanted of them, so every morning he would go down to the compound and study them for a while, observing their movements and behavior. He would then decide whether or not to shoot them on that day. Every time that he said okay we had a successful day with them, and the one time when they were used against his advice they did nothing. It was quite extraordinary.

A supposedly trained lion was produced for Columbia's *Safari*, shot as an interior at MGM Studios. The walls of the set were barricaded, the camera and crew heavily protected. The lion was introduced through an entrance at one end. One look was sufficient to realize that this animal would not perform. He was somewhat elderly and had a world-weary air of having done all this before. He lollopped in, slowly negotiated the barricade, retired to the middle, lay down, and promptly went to sleep. He was supposed to growl at our hero (Victor Mature). Nothing or no one could wake him up. The trainer was shouting his head off and poking him with a stick, but the animal did not even move. Eventually a stretcher was produced and three people manhandled this large beast onto it. Apparently he only woke up when he was deposited back in his cage. The comedy value was, unfortunately, not what was required.

Domestic animals are something else. A new cat food was being marketed, and the commercial for it was being shot in a studio in London. Six cats of varying hues were assigned to eat this delicious new product. Despite all entreaties and inducements, they would have none of it. Another half dozen were sent for, but to no avail. Eventually the small studio was awash with them. They were asleep on the girders, the floor, and anywhere else that took their fancy. You tripped over them when you made the slightest move. Fights broke out. The shoot was finally abandoned when it was discovered that two full bowls of food, which had been placed to one side, had been completely devoured, with the camera nowhere near them. In the event I believe that it was ultimately done as a cartoon.

Birds are even trickier. Pigeons were required to fly over the monster pack of Silk Cut cigarettes in a commercial shoot. The trainer had assured us that it would be no problem at all. He had not taken into consideration the heat in the studio caused by the lamps that I was using to produce a very high "key." When thrown in from the side, the pigeons would promptly reverse direction, away from the unaccustomed heat. Recordings of pigeons making mating noises were played. A bird impressionist was called in to lure them across. There was finally an attempt to "serve" them in, using a tennis racket. During the course of all this, the birds had taken their revenge, dispersing their droppings at will. This effort, too, was aborted at last at 2:.00 A.M. As we had started at eight o'clock the previous morning it could not be said that we lacked patience.

I do have one pleasant memory. Among the lion cubs in *Living Free* was a six-month-old named Francis. He was unfortunately cross-eyed and really took a fancy to me. The cubs were allowed to roam freely around the unit in order to get accustomed to us. Francis would seek me out and promptly sit on my foot. Even at that age he was no lightweight. He would then start purring like a rusty saw and lick my hand with what felt like a piece of coarse sandpaper. We had been told to make only gentle movements with the lions, so as not to alarm them. Extricating my foot very slowly was a painful experience, but when I had finally released it Francis would give me a reproachful look and walk away. This ritual happened every morning for some two weeks, much to the amusement of the unit.

I am quite sure that W. C. Fields was right.

# CHAPTER 15

~

# Harry Alan Towers

A whole book could be written about Harry Alan Towers. His varied and checkered career has spanned many years. He can certainly claim to be the most prolific film producer in the world. I worked on five of his films.

Harry had been a writer and producer for the first commercial radio station in Europe, Radio Luxembourg. From there he moved on to TV with Rediffusion and, doubtless by using all his numerous contacts, started producing his own films.

He frequently raised the monies for these in foreign parts, shooting the film in whichever country had financed it. He also rapidly became known for his propensity to be a little tardy in paying his bills but usually found the funds before things got too difficult.

I first met up with him in the early 1960s when he was making a film called City of Shadows in Salzburg, Austria. I had been warned about his not being too hasty about parting with money, but I had been asked by an old friend, who was photographing the picture and with whom I had worked a good deal, if I would operate the camera for him. So off I went.

It was a novel experience. Until then, virtually all our feature film interiors had been shot in studios, and here was Harry proposing to shoot in hotel bedrooms, inside houses, and in any other setting that he could acquire cheaply. It gave moviemaking a whole new perspective. Sets were dressed as we went along, with any props that came to hand, and Harry wrote the script on the back of an old envelope.

The actors, who were mainly German, had been part of the deal that Harry had struck in order to get distribution in Germany. The picture had already been partly made in Prague, but for reasons not disclosed (but one could guess) had suddenly been transported over the border to Austria. It was real do-it-yourself moviemaking.

An open sports car was required, and Harry produced an ancient Czech Tatra with the paint almost nonexistent. Even he referred to it as the "Tatty Tatra." It badly needed a respray to be presentable and Harry, of course, knew where to get it done.

The car had to be parked in the foreground of the shot. The next morning it appeared in flawless white rather flat and dull. The reason was soon apparent. It started to rain, and gradually the paint ran off it as we were shooting. It was, of course, emulsion paint. Not one wit abashed, Harry got one of the local Austrians to park his car in the shot and we carried on. It got a bit complicated later on, when the same car had to be driven through a shot and neither the car nor the owner could be found. This didn't seem to matter, either. Another white car was found that bore no resemblance to the original. Harry merely opined that if anybody in the audience noticed that, then the plot was failing to grip them. Needless to say, a lot of people noticed it.

The great thing about Harry was that at no time was he particularly fazed, and he was nearly always cheerful and amusing. In fact, he was very likable.

What eventually became of *City of Shadows* I never knew, but doubtless it was shown somewhere to some unsuspecting cinemagoers. It certainly did not seem to hinder Harry's career.

After that I didn't hear from him until six months later, when I received a call from Martin Curtis, the cameraman who had photographed the picture in Austria, to say that Harry had offered him two back-to-back pictures to be made in South Africa, and would I like to attend? So off we went to Lisbon to shoot a sequence for *Mozambique*, thence to Durban via Johannesburg.

Harry's distributors had insisted that the films be shot in Cinema-Scope, but the budget could not sustain that. Instead he opted for what was known as the "poor man's CinemaScope," Techniscope. This system had been devised and developed by the Technicolor company, and it did have certain advantages. The camera movement had been adjusted from the normal four-perforation to a two-perforation pull-down, and the camera gate was masked off to half its normal height but retained the full width. This produced the same ratio, 2.33 to 1, when shot with normal backing lenses, and no "squeezing" was necessary. It also enabled a thousand-foot roll of film to immediately become twice as long, as the result was effectively getting two frames for the price of one old one. Techniscope's main disadvantage was that the smaller negative area, when projected, produced a slight loss of definition. But once again, there was no immediate comparison, so the quality was acceptable.

The camera gate had also to be kept scrupulously clean, as there was now a fine frame line between the images and any small foreign body or a hair would be magnified on the screen. But whatever its technical drawbacks, it was an extremely economical system for the producer, his negative and processing costs immediately cut by half. And no extra equipment to hire. This suited Harry's budget nicely.

He was on the plane with us to Lisbon, busily scribbling the script on odd bits of paper, but disappeared ahead of us to South Africa, doubtless to make a further deal or two. Apparently the financing was coming from there, in accordance with his usual method. The cast was mainly German again, the only "name" being Hildegarde Neff. The male lead was the American, Steve Cochran. He was already installed when we got there, judging by the number of young ladies around.

Never one to waste time, Harry was there to meet us on arrival at the airport and immediately took the senior members off on a quick round of the various locations he had chosen. Although it was the South African winter, it was very warm, and after the eight-hour flight we were a trifle jaded. The reconnaissance expedition was a whirlwind tour around Durban and its environs, and we finally got to the hotel for a shower and refreshment some three hours later.

We started shooting the following morning in the hotel ballroom, sparsely dressed in Harry's usual style. His organization, while quite good in general terms, lacked attention to detail. Consequently, although we had the set, the actors, the lamps, and so on, certain important props were missing. People were dispatched in all directions, Harry himself rushing hither and thither. At last we were all ready. But shooting was further delayed by the arrival of the hotel manager, demanding to know why we were using his ballroom to shoot in. The trifling matter of obtaining his permission had apparently been overlooked.

Hotel managers being child's play to Harry, the man's arm was taken affectionately and Harry, talking animatedly, led him away, appearing five minutes later and instructing us to proceed.

The first two weeks went off without problems, Harry coming and going to unknown places. At the beginning of the third week I came down into the foyer of the hotel to find the entire crew and the production manager having a heated conversation with the hotel manager. My crew announced that they had been unable to load the cameras, the equipment room being locked and the key not available. Once again, Harry had neglected to pay the bill, which was already a week overdue. And nobody knew where he was. So we retired to the lounge and drank coffee and waited.

Harry appeared an hour later, demanding to know what was going on. He had been out on the location already, waiting for us to arrive. On being apprised of the situation, he laughed and said, "Oh, that!"

A few minutes in the manager's office and all was well again. He came out muttering, "Don't people have any trust anymore?"

We proceeded from there with no further hindrance from the management. For the moment at least, all was well.

A certain amount of further consternation requiring more of Harry's diplomatic skills arose when certain intimate articles of ladies underclothing were discovered flying like flags from Steve Cochran's window. Once again the management were mollified, but we wondered how much longer their patience would last. Harry had foreseen this and hurriedly moved Mr. Cochran to another hotel.

In pure terms of making the film, we were proceeding smoothly enough.

"El Sombrero," as Harry had been nicknamed, had a habit of disappearing and then popping up again like the Demon King in a pantomime. We amused ourselves by trying to guess what he would be wearing each time he reappeared. He seemed to possess only two suits, one blue and one brown, so small bets were laid accordingly. Then he fooled us all by turning up sporting a gesture to the warm weather made out of what appeared to be fawn sackcloth. This was obviously his tropical kit. The tie, as always, was neatly held in place by the obligatory gold tie clip.

The plot of *Mozambique* escapes me, but it was basically a thriller, with a slight air of *Casablanca*. Harry was not averse to a little thinly disguised plagiarism.

Having used our current hotel for as much as the story demanded, Harry moved us to another, doubtless just ahead of the management's asking us to leave. This new venue was right in the center of Durban and more accessible to both our locations and our social life.

At this point Harry's mother arrived. She insisted on visiting Harry for short periods wherever he was working. This did complicate things a little for him in Durban, since his girlfriend was already in residence and the mother was ignorant of her existence. The girlfriend, whose name was Helga Stoenemann, had appeared during our Austrian venture. Harry called her "Schnitzel." The arrival of mother meant that Schnitzel had to depart, and for the next two months Harry's women came and went alternately.

When Harry's mother was there, a close watch had to be kept on her because she had an addiction to horse racing, and there was a racetrack in Durban. We frequently witnessed her sneaking down to talk to the Indian hotel reception staff who would place her bets for her. You could see Harry getting more concerned by the minute.

*Mozambique* was eventually completed, the last dailies cleared by the laboratories in London, and we moved on to *Coast of Skeletons*. Once again Harry was busily scriptwriting this tale of shipwreck, murder, and general intrigue. The plot was actually about Southwest Africa, but Durban would have to be mocked up to resemble it. A small unit was dispatched to Southwest Africa to get the necessary establishing shots and general atmosphere material. We contented ourselves with using the coastline around Durban.

One day took us to a nearby beach to shoot a small sequence in the surf. Harry appeared to see that we were getting on with it, clad in his stylish tropical gear. Seating himself in a deckchair, he commenced reading a book. I inquired what it was, to be informed that it was a Dr. Fu Manchu story acquired from the Durban public library for the princely sum of ten cents. It transpired that he had discovered that the author, Sax Rohmer, was just out of copyright, and Harry thought that he might film some of the stories. And he eventually did.

I thought it highly unlikely that the public library would ever see the book again, but he subsequently told me that that he had returned it and charged the ten cents down to research.

The next day we were shooting at the bottom of a cliff face outside the town. Somehow the location had been confused with a similar one farther down the coast, and as we prepared to set up the camera, Harry appeared at the top of the cliff, waving his arms about, and then started running down the steep cliff face. Halfway down he slipped and described a cartwheel, landing on his feet again and still running. He also retained the script, which was fixed under his arm. Breathlessly he told us of our mistake and immediately scuttled back up the cliff and disappeared.

We repaired to the correct location some three miles back down the coast road. Halfway there, our large electrical generator thundered past in the opposite direction. Obviously someone else had been misinformed. On arrival at the new location, we informed Harry of this and he promptly set off in pursuit. He met the generator a mile up the road, turned his car around and followed, only to see it returning another half a mile on. In despair he arrived back at the location, swearing that "That bloody 'genny' has done more useless miles than an Olympic gold medalist!" It eventually caught up with us, Harry's intended admonishments rendered pointless as the driver only understood Afrikaans.

I had instructed my bank manager to inform me if payments were not received into my account. To date all had been well, but a letter arrived telling me that nothing had been received for two weeks. I took Harry to one side. "Don't worry, dear boy! Don't you trust me?" To this there was no answer, and a check was duly promised. It arrived next day, and I looked at it dubiously. It looked as if it had been handmade and was bearing the insignia of the Bank of Nova Scotia. I had never heard of it. The address was in Kingsway, London. It was immediately dispatched to my bank, and a phone call three days later assured me that it was genuine. Only Harry would have an account in a bank nobody had heard of.

Apart from a small skirmish with the manager of our new hotel, things proceeded in good order. Harry had disappeared once more and was rumoured to be in Johannesburg, doubtless conducting further business. We soon found out what it was all about. He had discovered that one of the highest box office winners of that year was *Flipper*, the story of a dolphin. He returned in high good humor, obviously with more funds, and announced that we were going to make *Sammy the Seal*. We were finishing *Coast of Skeletons*, and he assured us that the new epic could be shot in three weeks. The pencil and envelopes appeared once more and the script began. A week later we began shooting.

Harry had been far from idle in Johannesburg. Among other things he had arranged with the zoo there to provide us with a seal, complete with lady keeper. They duly arrived on a beach at Umslanga Rocks outside Durban. The crew were unpacking the equipment as a lorry with a small tank on it drove onto the beach. As we watched, a large grey seal flopped out of the tank. It shuffled down to the water's edge, took a long look, and dived in. It swam strongly out and disappeared from sight. The lady keeper was distraught. We looked at Harry. As usual, he was not fazed. "Oh, well," he said. "I suppose we'd better get another one." Two days later the replacement arrived and was kept well away from the water. The lady keeper had the air of someone who would have to work for the zoo for a long time in order to pay off the cost of losing the first seal.

*Sammy* was really a children's film à la Disney, and the two leads were a boy and girl about ten years old. Unfortunately the new seal was temperamental and seemingly disliked them. If the little boy stood next to him he usually got bitten, so whenever possible a stuffed seal was used; otherwise we could not have continued. This presented some difficulty with the shooting, since it often seemed very obvious that the seal was not real. Some years later, on meeting up with Harry again, I asked him how the film had been received. He did say that his German distributors had actually asked if the seal was stuffed. He said that he told them no, but some of the actors were. That was Harry.

Even for Harry, this was do-it-yourself filmmaking at its worst. The hastily written script had large holes in it, and on being questioned by the director, Harry would mutter, "Well, do your best, do your best," and disappear. It was one of his favorite expressions whenever a knotty problem arose. The story was really made up as we went along. So, what with a bad-tempered seal, two undisciplined children, and a nonexistent script, things could have been better. Somehow we managed to get the required screen time and left it to the unfortunate editor to do what he could with it. He, too, must have endured many chants of "Well, do your best, do your best. . . ."

Disaster struck on our last shooting day. The clapper boy had been carrying the viewfinder as we changed setups. One of the locals had been sent to fetch the director's script, which he had left behind. Running back with it, he collided with the clapper boy and the viewfinder was sent flying, landing on a large rock and shattering the optical system. It was useless.

A replacement could be acquired from Johannesburg, but that would take a day and we had to continue shooting. Our still photographer had a Leica camera with a small Vidomcrome viewfinder, which I borrowed and lashed to our camera with the aid of the indispensable "gaffer" tape (without which, it was alleged, the film business would not survive). It fortunately had a center cross-marked on it, so at least I was able to have an image of sorts to work with. We managed to finish the day's work with it, but I was very glad to get the replacement next day.

There had been another slight problem at the finish with settling the hotel bill, so Harry could keep his hand in, but we left with no hindrance.

After returning from South Africa I heard no more from Harry for over a year. Then at 2:00 A.M. one morning the ringing phone woke me. He said, "Could you be on a plane to Hong Kong at ten o'clock this morning?"

"I'm afraid not, Harry. I'm right in the middle of a picture at the moment."

"OK, then." He rang off. He had, in fact, started shooting his *Fu Manchu* series.

Another couple of years went by, and in 1969 we met again. A director and producer I knew well were collaborating with Harry to make a film in Spain with the strange title *The Night Hair Child*, starring Brit Ekland, Hardy Kruger, and Mark Lester. It was to be shot by an entirely

Spanish crew, but the director insisted that I should be the camera operator. He obviously needed an aide among all the Spaniards. So, bracing myself for another dose of El Sombrero's unique brand of film-making, off I went again. As can be imagined from the cast, Harry had moved up a bit to a larger budget for the production. This time, and in accordance with his usual custom, the majority of the money had come from Spanish backers.

On arrival in Madrid I was installed in a fairly plush hotel that turned out to be owned by the Spanish Mafia, the Opus Dei. Normally this would have been of little matter, but after a week there the manager stopped me as I was leaving the building. Harry had once again omitted to pay the bill to date. This time I had to sit in the lounge while he was summoned. The usual sketch took place. By this time I could have written the script myself. Harry arrives, places arm around manager's shoulders, exits right toward the manager's office. Pause of approximately five minutes. Enter Harry with manager, trailing behind, who makes a gesture to the doorman to let us pass. Usual ad lib mutterings from Harry as to the lack of trust, etc., etc. The only thing that slightly concerned me was that, if this happened again, the thought of being in the hands of the local gangsters was none too pleasant. Fortunately, it never came to that.

The production itself went smoothly enough after we and the Spaniards settled in with each other. The experienced actors were easy to work with, and for once Harry's organization seemed to be in order. As usual, he kept disappearing from time to time, but left in charge a Spanish near clone of himself, one Vincenze. He had been trained well. Things that needed answering immediately or required decisions were dealt with by a combination of "Yes, it's all in hand" and "Do your best, do your best."

Harry was his usual friendly self, and we had a few chats about his past productions. He certainly had no illusions about the general quality of his earlier works and was very amusing about them. He agreed that few (if any) of his scripts were destined for the Hall of Fame.

The higher budget seemed to have a beneficial effect on his D.I.Y. approach. *The Night Hair Child* continued in good order, with none of the problems that had been experienced in South Africa.

I left Spain just before Christmas of that year, having found a col-league to take over from me. When approached to work on Harry's film

I had already contracted to go back to Kenya to do *Living Free*, the sequel to *Born Free*, and it was understood that I would be unable to finish his project.

That was some years ago, and I have not heard from Harry since. Harry possessed the gifts of resilience and resourcefulness. At one point of his career he was deported from America but has since been back somehow, and gotten away with it. One has to admire his ingenuity. From time to time I hear of his exploits, which do not appear to have changed much. He is still out there somewhere, taking hotel managers affectionately by the arm, etc. And sometimes I fancy I hear a voice saying, "Well, do your best, do your best. . . ."

He is nothing if not unique.

# C H A P T E R   1 6

## ~

# Aircraft and Ireland

Being run over by an aircraft is not the sort of thing that happens to many people. It happened to me at Shannon Airport in Ireland when shooting *A Letter Is Waiting* for MGM. The story was based on the true situation of a young American who had written to his girlfriend in Ireland breaking off their engagement. He has second thoughts, and decides to intercept the letter by flying his own light aircraft to Ireland. We were to film his plane landing at Shannon, out of fuel and only just making it. As it descends, a large DC-8 freighter is taking off, and our hero's aircraft narrowly misses it, passing underneath. The light aircraft, an Auster, was piloted by a stunt flier, John Crewdson. We had four Arriflex cameras, one in the DC-8, one (unmanned) in the Auster, and the other two mounted in camera cars on the perimeter track parallel to the runway. The point of being mobile was to be able to follow the Auster if necessary to get it actually touching down and seeing the DC-8 just missing it. My camera was shooting toward the Auster, the other toward the freighter. I instructed my driver to keep his engine running.

The first take was not successful. It was essential that I have both the aircraft in the picture at the same time, to capture the nearness of the collision. I followed the Auster as it came down, but the freighter took off too soon and was too high for my picture. A hurried conference was held with the director, Andrew Stone, who was in the other car, and we regrouped and tried again.

This time it worked perfectly. The freighter appeared in exactly the right place in my frame, the Auster passing perilously close to it. I continued following the Auster as it touched down. Then, as I looked through the camera, I saw it slew through 90 degrees and come straight toward us. It subsequently transpired that the jet backdraft of the freighter had turned it, because it was on a dead stick (no engine). The inclination of the Auster was such that John Crewdson could not actually see us and at first he did not realize that he was coming straight at us. The wing tips of the plane were disappearing out of the sides of my picture, and I saw that it was almost upon us. I shouted to the driver "Go!" Unfortunately, during the lull between the first and second takes he had switched off and not restarted it. We could not move.

As the wingtips swept over the car, I shouted, "Get out!" and dived beneath them, hitting the hard tarmac. Looking round I saw the Auster crunch into the car.

Fortunately it had almost stopped by that time. The director of photography, Dave Bolton, who on the first take had been in the other car but had joined us for the second, had fallen to the ground and was rubbing his eye. I realized that his glasses were smashed and some of the glass had gone in. I shouted at him to stop rubbing his eye, and through all the chaos he miraculously heard me. Unfortunately I was not soon enough to save the eye completely and he was subsequently only partially sighted. He was also concussed, as indeed was the director, whose wife also happened to be in the car and sustained a broken knee. My injuries consisted of only a grazed arm and a pair of torn trousers, but we were all badly shaken.

But the shot had been a success, and despite his slight concussion Andrew Stone wanted to carry on shooting, although he was obviously far from all right. The ambulance took far too long to reach us (which raised an inquiry about efficiency at an international airport such as Shannon). Stone was treated on the spot and insisted that we carry on after the injured had been taken to hospital. Which we did. Not an experience I would wish to repeat, all in all.

There was a period when I seemed to be always in Ireland, a situation I thoroughly enjoyed, apart from the aforementioned incident.

*Flight of the Doves* was a family tale of two Liverpool children escaping from a wicked stepfather (played by Ron Moody) and endeavoring to reach their grandmother (Maureen O'Hara) in Galway, during the course of which they are helped by a kindly friend (William Rushton). This took us in stages across the entire width of Ireland. Right in the middle is Athlone, where we shot for a week, staying in a local hotel.

The hotel was run by a couple who had worked in the theater at some stage in their lives, and, of course, loved our invasion. Although I wasn't over sure of that after a week of our custom.

The lady of the house had also been a pit pianist for the silent cinema in her young days and was prevailed upon by Willie to give us a concert of the tunes she used to play. Willie and Barry Guigman (an Irish actor also in the movie) would appear in costume and enact the plot of the film she was accompanying. Their grand finale was *The Perils of Pauline*, which involved tying the heroine to a railway line, as a train approached.

For this an unsuspecting waitress was conscripted. As it meant throwing her to the floor and trying to tie her up, she was understandably more than a trifle apprehensive. She got an attack of the giggles as they managed to tie her to a stretcher simulating the railway line and then carried her off. Willie reappeared to pass the hat round on her behalf for being so sporting. The rest of the hotel clientele lapped it up, and I think the management would have liked to keep it as a permanent cabaret, as it was obviously good for trade. The climax of the evening was provided by the chef who appeared in his working costume leading a young goat. Both he and the animal were covered in lipstick. The ensuing dialogue can best be left to the imagination.

I have often wondered who makes up the many Irish stories we have all heard. There was no need to invent the tale of a cameraman friend of mine who, when driving to an Irish location for *Alfred the Great* on a fine summer's morning, found himself at a railroad level crossing. The barrier arm on his side was closed, but the far side open. There appeared to be no one around. After ten minutes or so, just as he was getting rather agitated, a small leprechaun of a man shuffled around the corner.

On my friend inquiring as to why one arm was up and the other down, there was a pause as he scratched his head. "Ah, yes sor, Oi know!" he exclaimed. "Yer see we're half expectin' a train!" To that, of course, there was no answer.

Our last location on *Flight of the Doves* was on the far west coast at Galway. My wife, who had been with me for a couple of weeks, had to return home and get to Dublin for her flight. After the day's shooting I drove her there, grabbed a couple of hours' sleep at the airport hotel, and set off again at 5:30 in the morning. I had always assumed that, as Ireland was primarily an agricultural country, there would be plenty of people around abroad on a early summer morning. I saw no one until I was about halfway back, passing through a small village. There, lying in the middle of the road, was a body, which I nearly ran over. I pulled up in some alarm and went across. To my relief the figure stirred and asked if I would give him a lift home, "which is only a mile or so down the road." Despite the fact that he reeked of whisky I bundled him into the car, asking him to tell me when we got there. He promptly went to sleep and snored loudly. After a couple of miles I woke him up.

"Are we there yet?"

He peered round and said, "You've bloody passed it! It's half a mile back!"

Feeling that his drunken belligerence called for carefully diplomacy, and there still being no one else in sight, I ran him back.

He stopped me after barely a quarter of a mile and got out without a word of thanks. I quickly turned the car round, noting that there was no visible habitation. As I looked in the mirror I saw him running after me doubtless to tell me he had made a mistake. I pressed on to Galway and saw not another soul until I arrived there.

I have been reliably informed since that there are more Irish living in New York than there are on the whole of Eire. After that I could believe it.

At the completion of the film I was asked by our Irish clapper boy whether I would like a drop of the illegal brew, poteen. He produced same in a grubby bottle, assuring me that this was of the very best quality. I hate to think what the worst quality was like, as this was the only bottle of alcohol that after an initial taste remained untouched in my house for over a year. All attempts to pass it off on friends or guests in various forms were of no avail. It was eventually used to clear a blocked drain which it did most effectively.

Ireland continued to produce its own brand of magic. On a different occasion I was scouting with the director for locations on a commercial. After a long and fruitless morning we found ourselves in the small village of Shannonbridge at noon. The director said he could use a beer, and there, hard by, was one of those general-stores-cum-bars found so frequently in Ireland. We walked in to find it deserted. I suddenly remembered that between the hours of 12 noon and 1:00 P.M. was the Holy Hour, when bars were normally closed for "maintenance" (i.e., removing the drunks and sweeping the floor). At that moment the proprietor appeared. I apologized for our presence, explaining that I had forgotten the time and knew that he would not be open for business for another hour.

"That's very good of yer ter remember, sor. Would you care for a drink while yer waitin'?"

I did not return to the Emerald Isle until two or three years later, this time to photograph a documentary retracing the journey of St. Brendan, who was believed to have sailed to America in a banana-shaped leather boat, circa A.D. 800. He supposedly started off from the Dingle Peninsula, where David Lean had shot a sequence for *Ryan's Daughter* on the nearby Inch beach. As a short preamble, we needed to shoot a sequence of the surrounding terrain and asked at our hotel where the beach was. A local gentleman, overhearing our conversation, said he would take us there in the morning. We set off and drove some five miles along the coast until he said, "That's it, over there!," pointing to a small beach by the road. We had all seen *Ryan's Daughter* and this beach looked nothing like it. We said that surely the film had been shot somewhere other than here, to which he replied, not one whit abashed, "Oh, that would have been Ryan's other daughter, to be sure!"

We never did find the real thing, as time would not allow.

# CHAPTER 17

~

# Things Weren't All Right on the Night

Special effects is one section of filmmaking that has traditionally been viewed with a certain amount of suspicion and caution by technicians. It is usual to ask the experts where the explosions, etc., are due to take place and where they consider it safe to put the camera. Past experience has taught cameramen to double the alleged distance from the effect, barricade the camera (and self), and make sure that there's an escape route. I have nearly finished up wearing odd flying objects, and on one occasion—on *The Italian Job*—half a motor car. So one was always a little wary.

Take, for instance, the blowing up of a telephone booth by the Berlin Wall on the lot at MGM for *Casino Royale*. The plot was that Orson Welles goes into the telephone booth and picks up the receiver, and that causes the whole booth to explode.

Our effects man was taking no chances on its being unspectacular. The camera was some fifty yards away, underneath a rostrum, the front covered just enough to leave a large enough rectangle for the lens. The crew dispersed themselves well behind the camera position, and we ran the camera.

The effect was sensational. It was not so much an explosion as a complete disintegration. After the dust had finally settled down we were treated to the ludicrous spectacle of a dummy, representing Welles, held upright by a length of tubular scaffolding. Of the Berlin Wall and the telephone booth there was not a trace. Several members of the crew who were in a supposedly safe place well behind the camera sustained minor flesh wounds from the flying debris. The protective board in front of the camera had pieces of plaster deeply imbedded in it, such was the force of the blast. You could say that the whole thing had been a trifle overdone.

It was a balmy summer's evening on the lot at Pinewood Studios. We were preparing to shoot a night sequence for *Carve Her Name with Pride*, a story of the wartime French Resistance. A large village set stood ready to be bombed by German aircraft—or, to be more exact, blown up by the special effects department. We had just arrived on the set, refreshments were being taken, and the only sound was the rustle of timesheets being made out. The camera equipment, still in its boxes, was being unloaded.

Special effects had been hard at it all day, rigging the village with explosives. The director was conferring with the head man as to when and where the explosions were to happen.

Having satisfied himself, he was discussing with us where to position the cameras. "Oh, by the way, Sid," he said to the special effects chief, "how do you fire them off?"

"Very simple," was the reply. "All I have to do is touch these two wires together like this. . . . " There was a series of shattering explosions as the village erupted.

As the noise and the dust died down, the calm voice of the assistant director could be heard. "All right boys. Wrap it up. Same call in a week's time!"

In Shepperton Studios we were shooting a storm sequence in the large studio tank for *The Guns of Navarone*. To simulate the storm there were wave machines, large aero-engine fans, and big tipper tanks loaded with water up in the gantry above us. We were on a rostrum in the middle of the tank, clad in rubber wet suits, and the camera was suspended from the gantry by heavy-duty sprung rubber cables.

The shot was of David Niven jumping out of the sinking boat into the raging sea. The full scale of the storm effects was activated, we rolled the camera, and the cue was given for a tip tank to discharge its load. Somehow the cue was misinterpreted and the wrong tank spilled out. It happened to be the one dead behind camera. It hit me fair and square in the back and catapulted me straight into the water.

I came spluttering to the surface and found myself next to David. He took one look at me, speechless, and said, "Well, go on then. You've got the first line!"

Freddie Francis, the only British cinematographer to have won Oscars for both monochrome and color photography, was shooting exteriors one wet, windy, and dark day in November. He was becoming increasingly impatient with the indecisive director, who was constantly changing his mind as the light worsened. At the exact moment that Freddie was about to announce that the light had finally gone, the director said, "I think I would like two cameras on this shot."

This was the final straw. Freddie replied with a deadpan face, "I'm sorry, John, there is not enough light for two cameras!"

The director accepted it without a murmur.

# CHAPTER 18

~

# Hungary and *The Golden Head*

I had worked with Jimmy Hill as a camera operator a year or so previously, when he had directed a small film called *Lunch Hour*. Jimmy had been very successful with a variety of subjects and had won an Oscar for a charming children's film he had made in Italy. He had been asked to do a film in Hungary; would I like to meet up and discuss it?

He explained that this was a subject he had wanted to do for some time and that it was basically another children's story. It had the strange title of *Milly Goes to Budapest . . . but Who Is Milly?*

But things had moved on from when the script was first written. It was at the time when the large-screen process called Cinerama was in vogue, and they were looking for new material. *Milly* had appealed to them as family entertainment. What had started as a little low-budget film about the theft of the Golden Head of St. Lazlo, one of Hungary's patron saints, to be shot in three weeks or so, had now developed into a large international production with a huge budget and a long schedule. Cinerama had used several different processes in the past to achieve their large-screen format, but this time they had decided to use the Technicolor Technirama system. This was a rather "cobbled together" method of producing the Cinerama format consisting of a Vistavision camera—the eight-perforation horizontally running movement—plus the "Delrama," a squeezing lens mounted in front of the backing lens. The old "three-strip" camera had been modified to produce this, and it came with the same "icebox" camera sound blimp and its equally heavy ancillary equipment. It was altogether a very cumbersome affair that had to be mounted on a twenty-two-inch geared (handle) head.

The director of photography was a young Hungarian with a fine track record, Istvan Hildebrand. He was not versed in the technique of operating this head and, as I was, it gave Jimmy the opportunity to ask for me.

In those days Hungary was still Communist-ruled, and as I had never been to a communist country before, I was intrigued to see it.

Budapest, standing on a huge bend of the Danube, has a long, arcane history and some fine Baroque architecture. A good example was the Margitziget Hotel, where I was staying. It was very old. However, in my room on arrival was a large bowl of fresh fruit, a box of chocolates, and a bottle of Hungarian brandy, courtesy of the Hungarian production company.

The crew were once again international. Apart from the locals, there were seven or eight Americans from Cinerama, an Austrian production designer, a French stills cameraman, and eight British technicians.

The hotel, realizing that they had many different nationalities staying with them, elected to put the relevant flags on the tables in the restaurant. Judging by the order of service, it seemed that the British were well down the popularity list, as we always seemed to be the last to be served. Even changing our flag for the Russian in the hope that it might speed things up was of no avail. Obviously the Hungarians had a similar opinion of the Russians.

The first day of shooting arrived. It has always been tacitly understood that the first day of any shoot is vulnerable. Everything and everybody are new; if you get through without anything untoward happening, it is always a plus.

Only one thing did hold us up, which meant a loss of one hour's shooting time, but it could hardly have been foreseen. The second shot of the day was from a baby camera crane. The weight of the cumbersome Technirama camera was far in excess of anything they had been used to, and they did not have sufficient counterweights to balance the camera. Inquiries at the studio revealed that there were no more there, either. People were dispatched, and eventually a small battered lorry bearing a load of various pieces of pig iron arrived. This did the trick, but it was plain that the Hungarians felt that they had been found wanting, and on the first day as well. I managed to mollify them a little by telling them that this was often "par for the course" on the first day of shooting.

After that things went well for the next few days. The mixture of people was beginning to gel together and a general rapport was felt all round. There had been a slight friction between us and the Hungarians because our method of shooting was different from theirs, but this had soon been resolved.

The second week commenced with us aboard a launch on the Danube. Once again, the weight of the camera had not been taken into consideration. The first shot was from the stern of the boat, and, as the camera was put into position, a heavy arc lamp was placed alongside. This tipped the scale of balance and trim of the launch. The prow rose out of the water and loose objects slithered down the deck. A concerted rush to the bow just prevented the stern from going under, but there was already an excess of water slopping about. In addition, this part of the river was subject to strong currents, and the boat started to swing about. An air of slight panic prevailed. The captain took over and managed to maneuver the boat to the shore where things were put to rights. As the chief cause had been that arc light, Istvan Hildebrand was asked if it could be not used or placed somewhere else. He did not take this well and went off in a huff. Despite this we climbed back on board and pushed out to midstream to continue. All was now ready to shoot, but no director of photography.

He could be seen on the bank, sitting on a seat and smoking a cigarette. A shouting match in voluble Hungarian took place. At length a rowing boat with the production manager aboard went off to fetch him back. From the boat we could see the two figures gesticulating wildly, and eventually they returned, Mr. Hildebrand still sulking. He had apparently taken the situation very personally. That evening Jimmy Hill and I talked to him and got him to relax. As Jimmy said, we could not have incidents like that every five minutes; the last thing we wanted was a temperamental director of photography. As I got to know him better I realized that he was extremely sensitive, and he subsequently admitted that he thought that we were questioning his professional expertise. It was all sorted out and my personal relationship with him improved.

Thus far I had taken all my evening meals in the hotel, but one night the Technicolor technician, the continuity girl, and I decided to eat out. It was difficult to select any particular place; from the outside they all seemed the same. Gypsy fiddlers all playing Monti's "Czardas," wandering from table to table. Hungarian goulash in abundance. And groups of earnest young men sitting at tables drinking wine copiously. It was like a scene from the *Student Prince*.

We were to learn that, in fact, they *were* all the same, both the menu and the music conforming to the State edict. The only difference seemed to be that as you got farther away from the city, the quality of both deteriorated. Oddly enough, this was our first reminder of the political situation. But next morning I had another taste of it.

I had called into the production office to collect the mail and was asked by the production manager if I had enjoyed the meal at that restaurant and the "nightcap" we had at another bar afterwards. He knew the names of both of them and exactly how long we had spent in each place. We then became aware that "Big Brother" had been watching us. I kept a wary eye open after that, but I never saw or heard anything suspicious. But we didn't like the knowledge that they apparently knew everything we did.

Coming back to the hotel one day I found the actor Lionel Jeffries, who was featured in the picture, deep in conversation with a man lying on a sofa in the lounge. "Come and meet a publican from London," he announced. The man in question seemed rather confused and not a little disheveled.

He turned from Lionel as I arrived. "Now, you can tell me. Where am I?"

A trifle taken aback and a bit amused I replied, "Well this is the Margitziget Hotel in Budapest. Where do you think you are?"

"Oh, my God! I'm supposed to be in Majorca!" He had been seen off by friends at the London airport, apparently, had had quite a few drinks, and had somehow boarded the wrong plane. How he had arrived at the

Margitziget he had no idea. Lionel thought this was marvelous and, as the different members of the crew arrived, went through the whole performance again. The wretched man had to stay the night—with a few more drinks—and when last seen was trying to explain matters to the hotel desk and get himself to Majorca.

By this time Istvan Hildebrand and I were getting on well, once he realized I was on his side and not part of an English plot to undermine him. Being a Hungarian luminary of sorts, he enjoyed a few extra privileges. He lived in an apartment in the old part of the city but also had a small cottage up in the Buda hills. He invited me up there to spend a Saturday night with him and some friends. His attractive girlfriend cooked an excellent meal, and then he produced a couple of bottles of *barask*, a Hungarian brandy made from plums. It went down very smoothly—in fact, too smoothly, as three of us finished off both bottles.

During the consumption of these Hildebrand told me about the system as it applied to filmmaking in Hungary. Most of it was the expected inefficient bureaucracy, but I was horrified to learn that if any of his films were thought by a committee not to reach a certain standard he stood a real chance of being demoted right back to being a clapper boy. He asked if this was the same in England. I explained that it wasn't, and he said he would like to work there. I hoped I was not going to be responsible for another dissident asking for political asylum!

The evening went on but eventually I remember making a rather unsteady journey to my bed and waking next morning with a heavy hangover. The others had fared no better. But they knew a cure for this, so off we went in Istvan's battered old car to a little café bar. They were obviously well known, and the owner produced glasses of a very dark liquid that I looked at suspiciously. "Drink it down in one," they exhorted. I did, and the aftertaste was ghastly. But it did the trick, and almost immediately I began to feel better and stayed for lunch. But I decided to eschew any more alcohol. My companions got straight into the wine. I had thoroughly enjoyed the occasion and it made for good public relations.

We had a day's shooting to do at Gyor, a small town on the Czechoslovak border. It possessed a lovely cathedral complete with a magnificent organ, which someone was playing as Jimmy Hill and I wandered in. Whoever he was, he was a brilliant musician. Bach's

Toccata and Fugue in D flowed over us followed by a selection of impromptus. Undoubtedly the fine acoustics added to the quality of the performance. As it ended, we applauded. This startled the player, unaware of anyone else in the building. He bowed deeply and left. We stayed on for a while just relaxing in the atmosphere.

The Hungarian producer was a former stills photographer, Alex Paal. On my arrival back at the Margitziget he was in the foyer having a loud argument with the American Cinerama producer. I met him later sitting at the bar. He was fuming. "They have fired me! But I refuse to leave until the end, whatever they say!" And he stayed.

We embarked on a week's night shooting mostly on or along the banks of the Danube. On the second night there was a very large area to photograph, and Hildebrand's lighting gaffer had produced a number of 20kw tungsten lamps. They were then a new innovation capable of producing a great deal of light. All in all there were thirty-six of them on board a series of barges strung across the river. A large number of generators had been acquired to drive this battery, which had taken the electricians all the previous day to organize.

We were about to commence shooting when shouting came from the river bank. I turned to see a barge in the middle slowly sink with six of the large lamps on board. As the barges were all chained together this had a "knock on" effect, dragging the others down in turn. Further chaos ensued from the fact that the lighting gaffer had sensibly shut down the generators, stopping the supply to the lamps but plunging us into Stygian gloom. Car headlights had to be employed.

These events decided us to abandon the night's shooting and endeavor to sort out the carnage by daylight. It had been a very costly exercise, and I wondered how the Hungarian insurance system worked, if indeed they had one at all. But we continued shooting the following night but in a much modified way. No large areas could be considered because the suitable lamps were still being dredged from the Danube. It took several days to retrieve them all, the strong current having swept them a long way downriver.

There had been very little viewing of dailies to date, but I had understood that all was going well. We had been shooting for about six weeks or so when I got a call from Jimmy Hill asking me to come up to his room in the hotel. It appeared that he had been fired by Cinerama, who were claiming that they were not getting what they wanted on the screen. It seemed that they had already sent for an American director to take over.

This was disastrous news, and I felt extremely sorry for Jimmy, who had become a friend as well as a colleague. It became clear that the decision had more to do with politics than with Jimmy's direction. Sadly, next morning he left, and Richard Thorpe, the new director, arrived. I had worked with him before on a Columbia picture in Africa, and he remembered me.

Cinerama had decided to stop shooting for two days while they reorganized a few things. Jimmy's dismissal had put me in a difficult position. I was on the picture at his insistence, as indeed was all of the British contingent, and we felt that we owed him some loyalty. I had already been approached by Cinerama, who had implied that it was fine by them if I wanted to stay and finish the film. I went out for a long walk along the Danube to think it through and make a decision.

The deciding factor was a phone call I had received from my wife the previous night. My son was then six months old, and she was more than a little concerned about his health, so I decided to return home. I explained my position to Cinerama, who were understanding and sympathetic. The next day I left for home, accompanied by the English producer, Alexander de Grunwald. During the first leg of the journey he was very nervy and uncommunicative. We flew from Budapest to Vienna, where we changed planes. The moment we arrived in Vienna he changed completely and became his usual cheerful self.

What dark secret was behind all this I never discovered. Possibly the covert state surveillance had bothered him. I had been none too keen on it myself. In many ways I was sorry not to have completed *The Golden Head*, as it had been renamed. No film technician likes unfinished business. As it was, within two weeks of returning I was on to another film.

# CHAPTER 19

~

# The Inscrutable Orient: Part 1

In 1976, just as I was preparing to go off to Greece to shoot the second unit of *The Greek Tycoon*, a story based on the life of Aristotle Onassis, the phone rang at 8:00 A.M. one summer morning. It was Ken Talbot, a friend and fellow cameraman, ringing from Hong Kong. He had a problem. He was working for a local company making TV commercials, but it was imperative that he return to England for three months. The company was reluctant to let him go unless he could find an acceptable substitute. What was I doing and could I help? I explained that I was committed to the Greek picture and would not be able to come for two months. That was fine, he said; that would work out nicely.

So in August of that year, having completed my stint in Greece, I enplaned for Hong Kong. In retrospect I realize that I was quite unprepared for the culture shock that was awaiting me. The journey was long, around fourteen hours of flying time, and even the spectacular approach to the old Kai Tak airport over Kowloon and under the washing lines did not initially make much of an impression. But the moment I landed and blinked into the heat, I knew I was entering a different world.

The heat and humidity, common at that time of the year, hit me like a wave. But what struck me most was the sense of energy permeating the atmosphere. And the smell. Whatever else Hong Kong is, it is certainly not the cleanest city in the world. Subsequently I was told a story about the comedian, Bob Hope, visiting for the first time. As he climbed into the limousine collecting him at the airport, he allegedly sniffed.

"What's that smell?" he inquired.

His companion grinned. "It's shit!"

Hope replied, "I know that, but what have they done with it?"

It had been understood and agreed that my sojourn was for three months, after which Ken would be able to return. During that time I shot about twenty commercials and realized that the standards were not terribly high and much was accepted both in scripts and production that would not have been passed in London. However, they were very appreciative, and I was sorry when my term ended. I had got to know Hong Kong a little and its peoples and I liked it.

There were other English cameramen working there, and one of them was Arthur Lavis, whom I had known in London and had last met in East Africa. We had met up a few times on the odd social occasion. I was back in my apartment packing my bags, as I was due to leave the following day, when the phone rang. It was Arthur. Did I have time to meet him for a drink at lunchtime? He had a proposition for me.

Much intrigued, I went down to one of our watering holes and was introduced to his Chinese boss, David Ho. The scenario was that Arthur had been offered a feature film to be made in the Philippines, but David would not release him without a suitable replacement. What were my plans?

It appeared that their company had a series of commercials to shoot on condition set by the advertising agency that they were to be photographed by a European cameraman. There was no immediate reason for me to return to the U.K., so naturally I said yes. I certainly did not visualize then that it was the beginning of a five-year stint in Hong Kong.

So I joined Dragon Films. David Ho had an English partner, Dorian Bond, who raised most of the European work. David brought in the Chinese, and they had two British directors. So began one of the most enjoyable periods of my time in the Far East.

At that time, Dragon was arguably the most successful of the commercial companies in Hong Kong. Most of the work was for accounts such as Coca-Cola, the Hong Kong and Shanghai Bank, Mars, American Express, and, as tobacco advertising was still allowed there on television at that time, Marlboro and Winston cigarettes. It was a fiercely competitive business, and I was frequently required to go to business lunches and meetings to help get the contract.

The international work started to emerge and Dragon was given the green light to do a series of commercials for Korean Airlines. We started off in Seoul for three days, then across the Pacific to Los Angeles. Alcohol, although available, was not encouraged on Korean Airlines. Consequently on this eight-hour flight the hostess could produce only four cans of beer. As there were four of us, they were soon dispatched.

On requesting an encore she informed us that all she had was a dram of gin. She then produced an extremely ancient bottle in which indeed there was only a dram. We tossed for it, I won, and it was duly poured out, with an equally small amount of tonic water. At the moment she placed it on my small seat table, we struck a patch of turbulence, the plane bounced, and the glass fell to the floor. We watched in silence as the last drop of alcohol on board soaked into the carpet. It was a long thirsty haul to Honolulu, the port of entry to the United States.

On arrival my colleagues made a mad scramble for the bar, as there was only a one-hour stopover. For economy's sake I was carrying in my hand luggage two rolls of unexposed film to be used in the United States. The Customs search revealed these. They were regarded with deep suspicion. I explained what they were. The two official's apparently harbored thoughts that they could be "blue" films, of which quite a lot had been smuggled in lately, they informed me. They wanted to open the tins to find out. I told them that if they did, they would ruin the unexposed film and that we would have to charge them for the replacement cost. This altercation took the best part of the hour, and by the time I had convinced them that I was speaking the truth and they reluctantly let me through, it was time to reboard the aircraft, with no time left to slake my thirst. That my companions had managed to do so admirably was no comfort to me. So on we went to Los Angeles.

It was my first trip to America, and I was looking forward to it keenly. We landed, only to find that some of our luggage, including a bag that contained some essential props and a few small photographic tools of mine, was missing. Fortunately it was found after a short delay.

Most of our shooting in Los Angeles was of a tourist-oriented nature, covering some of the main attractions such as Grauman's Chinese Theater, Knotts Berry Farm, the Farmers Market, Beverly Hills, Marina del Rey, and the beaches at Santa Monica and Malibu. I spent a lot of time gazing at places I had only heard and read about. Here at last, was the famed "Tinsel Town."

We were staying at the Continental Hyatt on Sunset Strip. I had read a report in the local newspaper (which, in retrospect, must have been false) that the murderer Charles Manson was due to be released. Coming down for breakfast one morning I was making my way down a narrow corridor which led to the coffeehouse when an outside door opened and a large bearded man with frightening eyes entered. To me he looked just like the picture of Manson I had seen in the paper. He stared straight at me. A little alarmed, I edged past him as he continued to stare. I looked back and his wild eyes were now glaring at me. It took two large cups of coffee to settle my nerves. The waitress, seeing my startled look, inquired. I told her as jokingly as I could what had happened, adding that it was obviously my imagination. To my horror she said, "Well, it could have been. He used to come here quite a lot before he was arrested!" I took no consolation from that!

After we finished our stint in L.A., I had to return to Hong Kong to shoot a commercial with Mark Thatcher, the son of the then British Prime Minister, who had just competed in the Macau Grand Prix. He arrived complete with bodyguard. The shooting went smoothly, and Mr. Thatcher departed. He went off to participate in a trans-African rally, got himself lost, and was reported missing for some days. This really worried the advertising agency, who had paid him an awful lot of money to appear in the commercial. Could they now show it, with him famously gone missing? Fortunately he turned up after about a week of wild speculation, resolving their problem.

For the third time in as many weeks I packed my bags, this time for Indonesia. On arrival I was introduced to Harry Baird, the chief of Ogilvy and Mather, the agency that had commissioned the films, and his charming Chinese wife. He took us down to his office and ran through the schedule with us. Jakarta was a hodgepodge of neat streets interspersed with slum buildings and areas of obviously great privation and poverty. At night many people slept in the streets; one could see them from the windows of our luxury hotel. I found this appalling contrast very hard to take. Harry merely said, "I know, but you get used to it." I never did. But as is often the case with Oriental peoples, they were generally uncomplaining and philosophical about their lot. It doubtless would not have made any difference if they hadn't been.

The Bairds were very hospitable to us during our stay and the shoot itself went very well. On the last day our producer, Dorian Bond, informed us that he had to leave for London next day to get married. This came as a complete surprise to us and was the first we had heard of it. So we decided to give him a stag party. We had been told that the old part of Jakarta, the original Dutch port of Batavia, was a lively and interesting area, so after an excellent dinner at the hotel we repaired there. Dorian did not have a particularly good head for alcohol, so some two hours later we decided to get him back to the hotel. As our party consisted of eight people, we had to take two taxis, Dorian coming with me.

Jakarta taxis are an alarming breed. They are always driven at breakneck speed, the suspension shot by the awful road surfaces, and the brakes virtually nonexistent. We proceeded along a narrow, very busy road, the taxis racing each other to see who could arrive at the hotel first. At this point Dorian thought that it would be fun to climb out of the window into the other cab, as we were now neck and neck. The two drivers thought that this was hilariously funny and were making efforts to go even faster, weaving in and out of the traffic. I managed to haul Dorian back before it got too serious. He, of course, was helpless with laughter. On being told the tale next morning, he went white and departed on the morning flight considerably hungover.

On return to Hong Kong something new had developed. Dragon had been asked to shoot a new commercial for American Express. But this time I was not going to photograph it but appear, by request of the agency, as an actor playing the part of an English banker alongside a tall Chinese also playing a banker. It was to be photographed by Arthur Lavis. This was altogether a new experience for me, appearing in front of the camera, and I thoroughly enjoyed it—not to mention the comedy dialogue from Arthur and the others, commenting on my appearance and performance. The agency had paid for me to have a lounge suit made (which in Hong Kong happened overnight). This also produced some ribald comments, as I had never previously worn one out there. I still have it; it has hardly been worn since then.

The final comment was from Arthur, who begged me not to take up acting professionally for my own sake. Personally (oh, vanity) I thought I was rather good. For some months afterward my picture was plastered all over town (even on the famous Star Ferry) exhorting people to use American Express. Quite a few friends visiting found themselves confronted with this on arrival and, having got over the shock, thought that I had made a career change.

From November to approximately the end of March the temperature and humidity drop to a more pleasant level. Clouds appeared in what hitherto had been a bald hot sky. This time of the year could be typhoon time. I never experienced a full "blow," but it was a fairly regular occurrence for the typhoon warning to be hoisted. This was the signal for people to stock up with provisions in case it developed into something nasty—and to make sure that there was enough alcohol, etc., for a Typhoon Party. When it got really rough people would not go to work, and a general battening down of the hatches would take place. Usually the center of the storm would not arrive, but there would be several days of extremely strong winds about gale force plus. I emerged from a car on such a day to have the door blown out of my hand and sail away into the harbor, and only just making it across the road before being blown away myself. Naturally it became a little exciting (not to say scary) and provided a certain diversion—including a few very interesting typhoon parties.

We had long known that Dragon Films was undercapitalized, but as we did an awful lot of work we had always supposed that the company was reasonably solvent. It appeared not. Dorian and David called us four Europeans to the office and informed us that they were closing down the company and going into liquidation. In two weeks' time we would be unemployed. This sadly ended a wonderful period of my Hong Kong sojourn.

I was now in something of a quandary, being thoroughly embroiled in Hong Kong by now and not particularly wanting to leave. Also I knew that the work situation in the U.K. was far from good, and after all, I had been away quite a time. I was established in Hong Kong, had acquired a good reputation, and made a lot of contacts. I decided to freelance, as indeed did my colleagues at Dragon. The next phase started.

The other commercial companies, of which there were five majors and a handful of smaller ones, knew me, of course. A freelance American director was going to the Philippines to do a hairspray shoot and asked me to photograph it. The flight time to Manila was only an hour and a half, but it was a very different world from Hong Kong. The city itself was still very Americanized from the war, with plenty of fast-food restaurants and bars, and some of the streets looked not unlike a typical Midwest American town. I was put up in the Manila Gardens Hotel in the center of the city.

The next day we went down to the local studio that was going to service our shoot with crew and equipment. Some of the lighting equipment was in poor shape. Most of it was very old and the bulbs inside them were black with age and did not produce anywhere near the amount of light they should have (or the correct color temperature). The company was quite aware of this but said that the import duty on any replacements was crippling. So I had to manage with what was available. On future occasions I smuggled small lamp bulbs and other items in for them.

As was quite common in the Far East, the locals were often unsure by your accent as to whether you were English or American. I didn't immediately realize that the Americans were not popular, and when I became aware of the local animosity I could only speculate about the reasons. It was to prove a little embarrassing on occasions, as the crew, so very friendly and helpful to me, were more than a little cool toward the director. I could only hope that it was not too obvious. Whether it was or not, I did not know, but it fortunately did not appear to affect our working relationship.

The crew were always cheerful and joking among themselves, which was nothing short of amazing when I later learned of their pay and conditions. Their remuneration was the equivalent of one pound sterling (approx. USD1.5) a day for all hours. They all seemed to have large families and how they managed to survive was inexplicable. One night I took the studio bus back with them, dropping them off at their homes, en route to my hotel. They lived in wretched places, some by evil-smelling streams with dead dogs and such floating in the water. The decrepit shacks had no proper sanitation or light. I felt rather ashamed at living in the comparative luxury that I did. But they never complained or seemed at all envious. On a later occasion I managed to be of a little help with their pay and conditions.

We wound up the shoot in fine style, the company giving me a farewell dinner at which I made a slightly bibulous speech thanking them for their contribution. Some of them came to the airport next day to see me off. Just before I left I learned something else. It appeared that I was not supposed to be there at all officially, because I had no work permit, although this was apparently considered to be of little consequence. It had been agreed that I would be paid in American dollars, the Philippine peso being of poor international value. These had to be bought on the black market. Naturally all of this was highly illegal and I was advised to split the money up into small amounts and distribute them in different parts of my luggage. I was assured that there would be no problem.

There, first thing I noticed at the airport was a large notice that stated that only the equivalent of one hundred American dollars could be taken out of the country, and any excess should be declared and handed over to officialdom. I was carrying considerably more than that. The sight of two armed patrolling policemen did not help, either. Having a guilty conscience made me feel that they were continually looking at me. Then over the public address system came the news that my flight was delayed for one hour.

I did the only sensible thing and retired to the bar, hiding myself in the farthest corner. After what seemed an eternity my flight was called. But there were still the customs and immigration processes to negotiate. A large forbidding lady inquired as to how much money I was carrying. I mumbled something about "fifty dollars or so." She asked to see it and fortunately I had around that sum in my pocket. She gave me a long, searching look and opened the suitcase where the rest of it was hidden. Visions of a Philippine jail came to mind as I gazed with a careless, nonchalant air at the ceiling. Once again, the time seemed endless.

Eventually she slowly said "OK" and left the case open as she went to deal with another customer. I strolled off as indifferently as I could manage. And then I was called back. In my agitation I had left my cabin luggage behind.

Fortunately the departure lounge also had a bar, so I retired there for a much needed restorative, my nerves feeling as if they had been scrubbed with a wire brush. I had loved working in Manila, but getting on that flight out was at the moment the best part of it.

On my return to Hong Kong I was asked to join a new company that already contained a few of my old Dragon Films associates. It seemed a good idea.

# CHAPTER 20

~

# The Inscrutable Orient: Part 2

This new company, Conic, seemed to be financially stable, unlike Dragon Films, and they also had a new studio, state-of-the-art equipment, and a video department. This last interested me, because I had no experience of shooting on tape. The chance came when the agencies asked me to photograph some of their lower-budget films. This was the cheap end of the commercials market, but it proved to be of great value later on.

By this time I had been working in Hong Kong for three years, and, apart from photographing the centenary fireworks display over the harbor, it had been an undiluted diet of commercials. I felt like doing something different for a change. David Ho informed me that he was going to codirect a Chinese feature film entitled *Superforce*. It was a kind of James Bond tale (but with a considerably lower budget, of course!). This would do nicely, I felt, as I had been dying to photograph a feature film once more.

I was a trifle disconcerted on discovering that the camera equipment was lacking in some essentials and that they were not over keen on supplying the number and type of lamps I required. Moreover, the schedule was a "stop and go" affair; the Chinese actors were not always available when we needed them.

I had made an agreement with Conic in order to do the film, but they had stipulated that I also make myself available to shoot commercials for them whenever I had a free day or days. It did become a little stressful occasionally, as after an all-night shoot I was sometimes required to be on a commercial set at eight the same morning. I realized that I had made a mistake in agreeing to this arrangement.

The movie itself was another matter. David and his codirector were frequently at loggerheads, and as neither of them had any previous experience, I had to spend a lot of time as mediator and diplomat as well as shooting the picture. The situation worsened after three weeks' shooting when the producer—who was the other director's brother—saw the discord between them and wanted to fire David. This put a great strain on my loyalties, as it was he who had asked me to do the picture in the first place. The atmosphere on the set was far from good, and the dailies were not very reassuring.

Matters were compounded by sudden overnight changes in the schedule, made without informing me, and on one occasion I had gone to an agreed location first thing in the morning only to find that it had been changed to an interior, and no lights were available because they had not been ordered for that day. This necessitated a three-hour delay until they arrived. I began to feel that I was wasting my time.

It was, in sum, altogether not very professional. And so it went on, the organization getting more chaotic. It finally came to a head when a supposed free day was changed to a shooting one—again without my knowledge—and I had been booked to do a commercial. I was generally far from happy and realized that I had to make a decision. I met up with the Chinese producer and explained my feeling about the overall situation. It was only then that I discovered that it was his first picture also and he patently had no idea how films were made. Consequently he did not understand that this was not the way to go about it and thought that I was being difficult.

Although I had never in my life considered such a thing before, I had no alternative but to resign; the situation was impossible. The whole project had become a sad disappointment, but it taught me never to get involved with a local Chinese picture again. To this day I am not sure that it was ever completed.

By way of a palliative, Blake Edwards and his crew were in town shooting a sequence for the current *Pink Panther*. A few old friends were involved and I was asked to shoot some material for them. It was a good feeling to be working with professionals again. After what I had just been through, I needed cheering up.

I felt that the time had come to reassess my personal situation. I had always had a rather loose arrangement with Conic, and of late had often been asked to shoot for other companies for whom I had worked in my freelance days. It was time to return to freelancing. Conic agreed, provided that they had first call on my services. This was fine with me, as it meant that I had the best of both worlds. So another new phase began.

An unexpected call came from a London company for a shoot in Japan. This was the one Eastern country I had not visited, so off I went to Tokyo via Japan Airlines and thence to Hiroshima by the famous Bullet Train. I had heard a great deal about the train, and it lived up to all expectations. At Tokyo station we were told to stand on the platform in an area marked with the number of our carriage. The train came in and stopped precisely there. It was the most spacious railway carriage I had ever seen and spotlessly clean. It started off noiselessly and was soon traveling perfectly smoothly around 120 miles an hour, we were informed. The wide aisles between the seats permitted the passage of trolleys selling hot and cold food, soft and alcoholic drinks, and newspapers and periodicals. A most enjoyable journey came to an end far too soon.

Our first location was in Hiroshima Harbor. At the time we thought that Japan led the world in shipbuilding, but we didn't see much evidence of it; the harbor was almost deserted. Even the water was littered with refuse, very unlike the clean ethic of Japan, and the giant cranes were still. The only large vessel there was the oil platform on which we were shooting. When asked, the Japanese were strangely silent about this. Perhaps their economy was not as strong at the time as it was made out to be.

By then it was lunchtime and we went off to sample some sushi, the raw fish that is a Japanese specialty. Sushi was quite a shock to European taste buds, but I eventually got to appreciate it. With the rest of the day free, we visited the site memorializing the consequences of the atom bomb dropped on the city on August 6, 1945.

It was a sobering experience. The awful power of the explosion was made graphically visible by the images etched on stone by the light of the blast, on view in the museum, which was set up exactly on the epicenter. Other exhibits consisted of a few pathetic rags and artifacts, as well as some horrifying pictures of some of the victims. From somewhere in the ruins they had found a clock that had miraculously survived, stopped at the exact time of the bomb's impact. We left without speaking, even our normally garrulous producer completely silent. The little museum had conveyed the dreadful horror of it all. Even an excellent dinner and a few drinks did little to revive our spirits. Only the next morning did we begin to feel more like ourselves again.

We had discovered that the Japanese were great ones for meetings. In fact it was common to have a meeting about having a meeting. What with that and the continuing courtesy of bowing to everyone all the time, we got the impression that we spent more time doing that than actually shooting. They were certainly very courteous hosts. The other impressive thing was the standard of cleanliness everywhere (other than the harbor, that is). Even inside a factory making tires, in which we shot a small sequence, it would have been possible to eat a meal off the floor.

The first day's shoot went well, and our Japanese clients insisted that we come to one of their clubs for a drink. These were exclusively male establishments, the only female being the waitress. They called for their own personal bottles marked with their names. It was mainly Japanese whisky, which they consumed at an alarming rate. I personally could not match the pace and retired, but two of the crew stayed on and next day swore that they would never do it again. The Japanese obviously had a lot of practice at this sort of thing and wore in good order, even asking for a breakfast meeting at 7:00 A.M.

On our last night in Hiroshima we decided to repay their hospitality and take them out to dinner. A first-class restaurant was recommended and around a dozen people attended.

Our friends did the ordering, the food was excellent, and a good time was had by all. We had already discovered that Japan was far from cheap by our standards, but the bill was staggering. We all emptied our pockets, but we still could not raise the price. The Japanese were politely ignoring our embarrassment. Then our producer remembered that the hotel was holding some cash for him in their safe. I was dispatched with all haste to get it, while the others stayed on under the watchful eyes of the management, who seemed to be getting a trifle worried by this activity. It took some time to reach the hotel, find the manager, and collect the money. There was only just enough. The last day in Japan was spent on the producer's credit cards.

To finish it all off in style, we flew back in a lesser typhoon, the plane virtually bouncing its way back to Hong Kong. It was a very uncomfortable journey, not to mention the damage to the nervous system.

I took stock of my situation once again. I had now been based in Hong Kong for four years after originally coming for three months, and I was starting to wonder if it was time for change. The local belief was that if you stay on "The Rock" for too long, it eventually gets to you. The oppressive summer heat and the occasional sense of claustrophobia brought about by the teeming population do tend to have a deleterious effect. After four years of virtually solid commercials, I felt I would like to get back to real filmmaking once more.

In the summer of 1982 I decided to return to the U.K. and see what was happening. The home business had been in the doldrums for some while, but I had heard rumors that things were picking up. Unfortunately it had not improved that much. I stayed for a month, enjoying the temperate climate—a marvelous change from Hong Kong's oppressive heat. But even though I had been absent from the scene for four years, not a lot had changed and not much was happening. So, a little reluctantly, I returned to Hong Kong.

Unwittingly I had returned at the right time. Things were buzzing. Quite a few of the production houses had been inquiring for me, unaware that I was not in the country. Almost immediately I was off once more to the Philippines for more beer and hair shampoo commercials.

That year was quite frenetic as I alternated between the Philippines, Indonesia, Korea, Singapore, and California. It seemed to me that I was always getting on and off airplanes, living in hotels and out of a suitcase. By now I knew Kai-Tak Airport backwards. Enough is enough. I was more than pleased to hear strong reports that the business had really improved by now, back in the U.K. Off I went, this time to stay.

But five years in Asia had been another milestone in my life and had greatly enriched it, both technically and culturally.

* * *

And so back to England and the vicissitudes of filmmaking in the U.K. Even after an absence of five years, the network environment had not perceptibly changed, and I was able to pick up some old contacts. It was good to feel a little more settled after a long period of globe-trotting—a chance to take stock. And to realize that during my career I had variously been: (a) run over by an aircraft in Ireland, (b) almost blown up in Morocco, (c) surrounded by a terrorist group in Africa, (d) tracked by the secret police in Hungary, (e) partially drowned in Malta, (f) lost in the snowy wastes of Norway, and (g) lucky enough to survive two plane crashes. I had even worked with Michael Winner.

# Index